LINUX
FOR
HACKERS

Tips and Tricks of Using Linux
Theories for Hacking

WILLIAM VANCE

Table of Contents

iii

v

Introduction

In the present age, technology has penetrated everyday human life, and its informative power has, in no small quantity, enlarged their level of creativity. This aspect of technology, otherwise known as 'Information Technology' (IT), is so vast that it cannot be completely explored at once.

A constant feature of technology has been its ability to evolve regularly. This explains the differences between outdated devices and new devices. There is definitely an improvement in the new devices, which makes the earlier produced ones outdated.

Years back, hacking was not so prominent as a field in IT, and even in this modern-day, there are still more discoveries yet to be explored in this field. It is the act of obtaining unauthorized approval into computer systems, hence, entailing a deep understanding of computer systems.

Hacking can be achieved through the decomposition of codes and passwords to bypass the security process of computer systems, thereby creating access to the systems. Gaining access to a password is obtainable through password cracking software applications.

It is important to note that hacking was not originally created for a negative intention; however, some individuals employ this to harm other individuals, firms, or companies. Their operations include fraudulent acts, violation of privacy rights, and gaining confidential information, amongst others. The purpose of this study is not to emphasize the negative use of hacking but to enlighten the readers on the tips and tricks of using Linux theories for intelligent purposes, which will be critically examined in the different chapters of this book.

This book covers such a large area regarding the tips and tricks of using Linux theories for hacking. This includes:

Hacking in the world of technology. In this chapter, the relevance of hacking, as a crucial area in information technology, will be examined in relation to the present world, otherwise known as the world of technology.

The emergence of Linux. This chapter centers on the origin of Linux and its operations to date.

Hacking devices. This chapter focuses on some of the hacking tools necessary for hackers to carry out their activities successfully.

Building a kali web server. This chapter illustrates the importance of a web server, how to create a kali web server and its operations.

Network management. A hacker should be proficient in networking. Therefore, this chapter explains how to interact with the network.

File manipulation. In this chapter, the processes of manipulating text files will be examined.

Scrutinization of wireless networks. A proficient hacker should be able to connect to another network device from his system. Thus, this chapter focuses on the operation of wireless networks.

Process creation and management. This chapter examines how to find, as well as manage processes.

Scripting. This chapter covers both the basics of bash and python scripting.

Software manipulation. This chapter examines three indispensable methods for adding software which are: GUI based-installation managers, alt package manager, and git.

Data compression. This chapter focuses on how to compress large files or multiple scripts into a smaller file.

Directory authorization. This chapter illustrates how to undersee and change permission on data. It also illustrates how to contrive directory and special permissions.

Anonymity and tracking security. This chapter briefly summarizes how to control the worldwide web anonymously by employing proxy servers, virtual private networks, the onion network, and private encrypted email.

Use and misuse services. This chapter focuses on accessing data with MySQL, setting up a web server with Apache.

Kernel module operation. This chapter illustrates how to change kernel workings and join new modules to the kernel.

Hashes, Passwords, and encryption. This chapter gives a brief summary of what passwords are, the function of hashes, and how they are connected.

It is also important for you to be familiar with some of the concepts and terms relating to Linux because you will encounter them frequently as you read through this book. A few of them will be briefly defined. They include directory, script, navigation, filtering, etc., terminal, shell, case sensitivity, root, etc.

- **Directory:** this is a structured listing of the names and features of the files on a storage device. It is related to a folder in the Windows operating system.

- **Script:** this is a file containing a list of user commands permitting them to be invoked once to execute them in sequence. Scripts can be executed using bash or python any other scripting language interpreters

- **Navigation:** navigating, especially through the file system, is a crucial task in Linux. Before you can execute anything, you need to first go through files, applications, and directories.

- **Filtering:** this is essential when we want to search for a word. It also enables us to take the output of a command and send it as input to another command.

- **etc:** in Configuration, this contains files that manage the starting up of programs.

- **Terminal:** this is the command-line interface. It is a device for entering data into a system.

- **Shell:** this refers to an operating system software user interface whose major function is to launch other programs and control their interactions.

- **Case sensitivity:** The Linux operating system, unlike Windows, is case sensitive. Linux users should be very mindful of how they use cases because a word may not appear to constitute any meaning in Linux if it is not written in the appropriate case.

- **Root:** this simply refers to the first user account with total access to the operating system and its configuration, found at the root of the directory system.

- **Command:** this is a directory to a computer program that acts as an interpreter to perform a specific task.

We shall now discuss the Linux operating system as well as the tips and tricks in using this system.

Chapter One

Hacking in The World Of Technology

In recent times, technology has evolved, especially in the area of getting things done easily for people. It has to do with the intellectual understanding of techniques, processes, and methods to accomplish a task or tasks.

Some peculiarities of this world of technology are increasing knowledge, and the quest for adequate security, especially dealing with vital information, files, or data. These are, in no small way, peculiar to hacking.

As people get more involved in technology, there is a pressing need for them to be educated, and especially for those working in companies, to ensure they are familiar with the cybersecurity threats and how to defeat them. Also, the quest for adequate security in this present age has immensely increased the need for hacking. Technology improvement has enhanced the performance of hackers to find cracks in corporate security systems, thereby granting them access to protected information.

In the introduction, we established that hacking is of two sides, depending on the intention of the hackers. It could either be done for a positive reason or a negative reason. However, the increasing rate of hackers with negative reasons is fast superseding those doing it for the positive reason; hence, the need for the latter to employ this same hacking to secure files or data. Fraudsters seek information for either private or business secrets. They also use it for monetary gain. When hackers focus on employees by manipulating their emails to seem like it is from a colleague within the same company or organization, which grants the hackers access to steal information or files, it is known as spear phishing

Hackers intensify the use of social media to engage themselves in identity theft plots. They lure people to transfer files through spiteful codes and passwords. Some personal information such as all or a combination of the following can go as far as granting hackers the opportunity to steal one's identity through social media:

- Name

- Age

- Date of birth

- Hometown

- Relatives

- Addresses

- Phone numbers

- Location updates

Another tricky way hackers can get information from individuals, sometimes, is when mobile devices are plugged into computers to be charged. In the present age, business owners are more involved in documentations, thereby giving them the necessity to operate in the cyber world. However, they have to be conscious of the fact that security measures must be put in place; hence, the need for professional hackers.

Those who hack for security reasons or investigate the attacks of hackers on a company's computer system, as well as provide proof of the delinquencies to the designated authorities, are referred to as hacking forensic investigators. As such, they are ethical hackers. Ethical hacking can further be divided into two: penetration testing to secure confidential information, and being a member of the intelligence agencies for your country. There is a high demand in these two critical areas, and this makes our study about hacking crucial, especially in this age. Penetration testing is so fundamental as companies are being established more frequently these days.

A penetration test is intrinsically a legitimate form of hacking to demonstrate a company's vulnerability of its systems and networks. Companies organize strategic vulnerability to evaluations to find out ways in which this occurs in their network, systems, and activities. However, companies should know that it is not everything that appears vulnerable that can actually be attacked. They must develop a system that can detect when there is actual vulnerability or not. This is where the penetration tester comes in. As a penetration tester, a fundamental conception of Open Systems

Interconnection (OSI) security structure is essential since hacking deals mostly with interconnected networks. Open System Interconnection is similar to the standards created by the International Telecommunication Union (ITU) to organize the task of providing security. Hacking is very crucial in a country's military and intelligence operations. We can envisage that hacking in this area will become more relevant in years to come. It is very relevant in spying, knowing beforehand, and prevent dangers coming.

Events, in recent years, have shown that living in the 21st century places a demand on individuals to understand how hacking works. Countries spy on one another to gain access to secrets, Cybercriminals are increasing on a daily basis, there are so many internet fraudsters, snoopers and investigators, thereby creating the need for security, which have also given room for penetration testing and intelligence agencies. To be an ethical hacker, one must possess an in-depth knowledge of how a computer operates. The evidence provided by the hacker is relevant for any of the following: bankruptcy, betrayal of employees, company investigation process, email scams, devaluation of web pages, breach of contract terms and conditions, and the likes.

Function Of Forensic Investigators
- Trace the malicious software and identity or signature

- Trace the location of the phone being used

- Regain deleted information or files

- Discover the device used to take a picture

- Discover when a file was accessed and altered

- Ascertain who accessed the network and who the fraudulent users are

- Draw out vital information from system memory

- Decipher what device generated the malicious software

- Break down passwords or codes on files, information or hard drives

- Trace what files the fraudster downloaded and the websites he visited

There are basically two types of attackers. They are passive and active attackers. A passive attacker may attempt to get some information and use that information to learn more about the system. However, it does not affect the system. An active attacker seeks to gain access to vital information to modify the operating system. The process of getting this information is referred to as *information gathering.*

In this chapter, we have studied how hacking is a great profession in the field of information technology with respect to the present age, otherwise known as the world of technology.

Chapter Two

The Emergence Of Linux

The Linux operating system was created on the 25th of August 1991 by the 21-year-old Finnish student, Linus Torvalds, who was an engineering student at the University of Helsinki, Finland. Collectively, Linux has been advanced over the internet by a host of programmers around the world. This operating system was one of the two operating systems that experienced an unfailing expansion in late organizations between 1996 and 1997.

Linus Torvalds was not as knowledgeable as Stallman in programming; however, Linus knew the influence and stability of the Unix operating system. He operated on this Unix OS and discovered that there needed to be an improvement on it. His repudiation of bad software boosted his interest in creating a complete operating system. Torvalds named this operating system 'Freax'; however, his friends thought the name was inappropriate. Therefore they renamed it Linux.

Before 1991, there had been some events that led to the creation of Linux. AT &T Corporation, an American multinational conglomerate holding company at Whitacre Downtown Dallas, Texas, backed out of the concept of a single-level memory. In 1969, Ken Thompson and Dennis Ritchie developed the idea of the Unix operating system and implemented them. Unix was generally adopted, altered, and duplicated by enterprises and even academic institution

Furthermore, the Berkeley software distribution (BSD) was created by the Computer System Research in 1997. However, AT & T filed a lawsuit against the University of California because of the Unix code that AT & T owned. This limited the growth of BSD. Richard Stallman invented the GNU project in 1983, intending to establish a free UNIX-like operating system. He further wrote the GNU General Public License (GPL). Intel discharged the 80386, which was the first x86 microprocessor with a 32-bit instruction set and a memory management unit with paging in 1985. Maurice J. Bach, a member of AT&T Bell Labs, published The Design of the UNIX operating system, which covered the System V Release 2 kernel, and some new features from Release 3 as well as BSD.

MINIX, a Unix-like system designed for academic purposes, was set up by Andrew S. Tanenbaum in 1987 to illustrate the principles portrayed in his book, *Operating Systems: design and implementation.* However, the intent of 16-bit MINIX was not well modified to the 32-bit features of the intensifying common and cheap Intel 386 structure for personal computers. The commercial UNIX operating system for Intel 386 PCs was too costly for private users. These elements and the defects of a commonly obtained free kernel necessitated the impulse for Torvald to initiate his project.

Since 1991, Linux has grown to be indispensable in the world of technology. The Linux operating system operates in a way that places a good deal of attention on the needs of the users, especially companies or organizations. Microsoft, another operating system, got popular because Torvalds did not intend to commodify his product. However, the Linux Kernel is developing for suitability and functionality because of its open-source outlook, which made it more accessible and potent. The software to be used with the kernel was created as part of the GNU General Public License, a free software license. Linux 0.01, which was the first distribution of the Linux Kernel, contained a binary of GNUs Bash shell.

Torvalds proposed discharging the kernel under the GNU General Public License. In December 1992, he published version 0.99 with the GNU GPL. Linux and GNU designers worked to incorporate GNU components with Linux to produce a largely working and free operating system.

The Chronological Development of Linux

Linux Kernel was publicly released on the 25th of August 1991 by Linus Benedict Torvalds, the first Linux distributions were invented in 1992, and the Linux Kernel was also relicensed under the GNU UPL. B by 1993, more than one hundred developers worked on the Linux Kernel. Through their operations, the kernel was adapted to the GNU environment, which invented a large spectrum of application varieties for Linux. Also, the oldest Linux distribution, as of 2018, was created. The Debian project was established during this period, and currently, it is the largest community distribution.

In 1994, Torvalds considered all parts of the Kernel to be fully developed. Therefore, he released version 1.0 of Linux. In 1996, the 2.0 version of the kernel was released. This gave the kernel more capacities to serve various processors at the same time with the use of symmetric multiprocessing (SMP), thus becoming a vital instrument for various organizations. In 2011, version 3.0 of the Linux Kernel was released. By 2012, the sum total of Linux server revenue exceeded that of the rest of the Unix market.

Version 4.0 of the Linux Kernel was released in 2015, and in 2019, the 5.0 version of the Linux Kernel was released.

Chapter Three

Hacking Devices and
Basic Commands In Linux

Hacking devices are software applications or the collection of software applications that assist hackers in exploiting computer systems, servers, networks, and web applications. This chapter covers the major hacking tools necessary to unravel the equipment employed in hacking.

Kali Linux is structured in such a way that it is not only meant for the public users but also experts penetration users or security auditors. It contains several tools for security-related functions. Presently, there are over six hundred tools available in Kali Linux, and more are being added frequently.

Before starting penetration testing, information gathering is an essential step to take. While gathering information, the hacker needs to exercise a lot of patience and concentration. There are different subcategories involved in the process: DNS Identification, DNS analysis, IP Identification, host identification, and so on. Some important tools are

- dnsenum

- Ghost Phisher

- Miranda

- nbtstat

- masscan

- Nmap

- The Harvester

- hping3

- iSMTP

- MSFConsole

- Maltego Teeth

- SPART

- DNSRecon

- Faraday

- dnstracer

- Dmitry

- dnsmap

- dnmap

- nbtscan

- Fierce

- Nikto

- Firewalk, etc.

For vulnerability analysis, some tools needed are Cisco tools, stress testing, fuzzing tools, and so on. The prominent tools are:

- BED
- cisco-auditing tool
- Cisco global exploiter
- Cisco torch
- BBQSQL
- copy router config
- Nmap
- Oscanner
- Sfuzz
- Yersini
- SidGuesser
- SIPArmyKnife
- DPBwAudit
- jSQL Injection
- THC-IPV6
- Sqlsus
- Sqlninja
- cisco-ocs

- powerfuzzer

- Openvas

Openvas is a vital tool for vulnerability analysis. You need first to download it because it is not, by default, installed in Kali Linux. To install it, use this code:

apt-get update && apt-get install - Openvas.

After it has been installed, change the username and password using this format: **root@kali:-# openvasmd --user=admin-new password=admin.**

To deal with wireless attacks, the following tools are needed: Airmon-ng, Airolib-ng, Airserv-ng, Wesside-ng, Easside-ng, Fern wifi Cracker, wifi Honey, Reaver, Blue log,gr scan, Kismet, Asleap, KillerBee, Airtun-ng, Crackle, coWPATty, Airdecap-ng, Airdecloak-ng, Aireplay-ng, Airodump-ng-oui-update, Airodump-ng, amongst others.

To guard web applications, there is a need for a coordinated platform for executing security testing for web applications. There are many tools provided by Kali Linux to execute this task. The tools function together to support the whole testing process. It begins with an incipient representation and decomposition of the attack surface of an application. It progresses to locating and exploiting security vulnerabilities. The essential tools for guarding web applications are: Apache users, BurpSuite, fimap, ProxyStrike, Nikto, Vega, FunkLoad, Grabber, Webshag, WBScan, Dirbuster,

Arachni, Maltego Teeth, Paros, sqlmap, jSQL Injection, Recon-ng, Uniscan, sqlninja, WebScarab, Webslayer, XSSer, etc.

Another category of hacking device is in WPS. The employment of WPS tools is called *stress testing*. Some important tools used in WPS are: FinkLoad, Inundator, DHCPig, iaxflood, mdk3, Termineter, inviteflood, SlowHTTPTest, THC-IPV6, ipv6-toolkit, and THC-SSL-DOS.

Exploitation tools are another category of hacking devices. This category of tools centers on web browsers. The rate at which webs are being attacked is increasing; hence, the need for these exploitation tools. To attack webs, fraudsters use browsers. The tools for exploitation include Metasploit, Armitage, BeFF, and Terminator. Exploitation tools are very crucial to penetration testing. Penetration testers search for computers that have vulnerabilities. There could either be a remote or a local attack. A remote attack occurs when you have no previous access to a computer. Your exploit needs to be transferred through the network. A local attack occurs when you have previous access to a computer that has vulnerabilities. Unfortunately, some attacks take place within a company by workers or the company's contractor. However, remote attacks are more difficult than local attacks.

Penetration testers need to convince their clients to sustain a well-secured information policy.

In a situation where a person deletes important files, an ethical hacker retrieves them. To perform this task, forensic tools are needed. They are used to preserve the data from the partition journal and make data recovery achievable. As we established in the introduction, forensics refers to the employment of science and technology in investigating and enacting facts and proof in an attempt to solve a crime. In Linux distributions, the most frequent details file systems are the ext3 and ext4 file systems. Data is stored in the partition's journal. Some of the tools in this category are:

- bulk extractor
- extundelete
- Foremost
- dStorm3
- explico
- Cuckoo
- DFF
- Pdgmail
- Dumpzilla
- Capstone
- Binwalk
- chntpw
- ddrescue
- Guymager

- RegRipper

- dc3dd

- iPhone Backup Analyser

- PDF parser

- Peepdf

- pdfid

and so on.

The devices for maintaining access includes:

- http-tunnel,

- Nishang,

- PowerSploit,

- shelter,

- webshells,

- Intersect,

- sbd,

- winexe,

- U3-pwn,

- Polenum,

- Cryptcat,

and so on.

Another major category of devices is Reverse engineering. These devices enable you to create varieties of malware families according to textual or binary models. They include:

- apktool,
- YARA,
- CaseFile,
- Javasnoop,
- Nipper-ng,
- jad,
- MagicTree,
- RDPY,
- Valgrind,
- dex2jar,
- diStorm3,
- Ollydbg,
- edb-debugger

and many more.

Sniffing and spoofing is another category of hacking devices. This category of devices deals with the shortcomings in network procedures. There are two subcategories in this category. The devices in this category act differently. There are many proxies in this category, and these proxies can be used to transfer a fraudulent inquiry for an attacker's site rather than the genuine host. These devices include:

- Burpe Suite,
- VoIPHopper,
- Sniffjoke,
- sctpscan,
- Yersinia,
- SIPp,
- rtpbreak,
- SIPArmyknife,
- Wifi Honey,
- responder,
- mitmproxy,
- THP-IPV6,
- protos-sip,
- xspy,
- zaproxy,
- Wireshack,
- DNSChef,

- iaxflood,

- inviteflood,

- hamster-sidejack,

- WebScarab,

- SIPVicious,

- rtpinsertsound,

- rtpmixsound

and many more.

Hardware hacking devices include:

- apktool,

- Arduino,

- smali,

- Sakis3G,

- Arduino,

- android-sdk

and so on.

In Kali Linux, some essential hacking devices are placed on top of the application menu. They are:

- Burpe suite,

- Metasploit,

- Armitage,

- Maltego,

- Beef XSS Framework,

- Faraday IDE.

Burpe suite belongs to the category of hacking devices that projects your web application. It creates a platform where the security testing of your web application is performed. It has several tools that work together to aid the whole testing process. Burpe Suite starts its operation with an initial and mapping and analysis.

You can perform penetration testing through Metasploit. Metasploit helps you to validate, find, and exploit vulnerabilities. It is one of the most effective tools for a penetration test. To be a penetration tester, you need to use some tools to carry out your activities effectively.

Metasploit is provided in the /usr/share/metasploit- framework directory. Also, it is necessary to understand Metasploit modules since nearly all the interactions with Metasploit occur through these modules. To find the modules, type:/use/share/metasploit-framework/modules.

Metasploit modules are arranged into different directories where exploit modules are referred to as modules that use payloads. *Payloads* comprise code that runs remotely. There are various types to explore, including firewall, backdoor, antivirus, mssql, MySQL and so on.

Another significant set of modules are called *auxiliary modules*. They indirectly institute a connection between a penetration tester and the target system. They also function in areas such as fuzzing or scanning, which help the exploit module.

Some systems still use the old windows version, which has so many vulnerabilities to Metasploit exploits. Therefore, a user who still subscribes to that old version is likely to be exploited.

Armitage is closely connected to Metasploit. It conceives the targets and proposes the needed exploits. The most estimable feature of Armitage is that it can reveal the post-exploitation structure in the framework. It can also secure downloaded files and data.

Maltego is another hacking device that has a special ability to display the complexities of points of breakdown, no matter how minute it could be. Undoubtedly there would be points of breakdown in a company, but this tool gives a clearer picture of the threat consciousness in their environment.

The Browser Exploitation Framework (BeEF) is a common penetration device that focuses mostly on the web browser. An attack usually starts from the browser and moves on throughout the system. BeEF, with the aid of clients-side attack vectors, permits a penetration tester to access the security threat.

Faraday is another hacking device that operates mostly for security auditing. A large volume of data is created during a security audit. The data can be examined, indexed, and distributed. This device started with a special idea of launching a multiuser penetration test IDE.

Important Commands In Linux

The **pwd**

This is a command used to find out the working directory you are currently using. Unlike the graphic user interface in other operating systems like the Windows and Mac OS that reveals the directory being used, Linux does not reveal its directory. Hence, while using Linux, before you will be able to navigate to another directory, you would need to know the directory you are currently using. The easiest way to do this is to enter the **pwd** command in your terminal. This would take you to the directory you are using.

whoami command

In Linux, the all-powerful system administrator is the root. When you have the root account, you can enjoy all the privileges of the Linux system, including adding new users, changing your password, and changing the privileges. The importance of this account is such that as a hacker, you can use the root account to prevent intruders from gaining access to your system. However, most times it is possible to be in doubt whether you are logged in as a root user or not. To find out which user you are logged in as, run the **whoami** command.

How to Navigate the Linux Filesystem

Mastering how to navigate the Linux filesystem from the terminal is very important. This skill helps you to find files, applications, and directories stored in other directories. Although using the GUI can allow you to see the directories easily, this is not so with using the command line interface. In fact, in CLI, to view your directories, you would need to run some commands. The easiest command to use for this is the **cd** (change directories). The Kali **cd** allows you to change the directories and move them up and down.

After using the **cd** to visualize the directories, to list the content of the directories, run the **ls** command. The **ls** command is not only used to view the contents of the directory you are currently using, but also to view the contents of any directories of your choice. To use the **ls command** for this action, write the name of the directory in front of the **ls**. For instance, to view the directories in the **etc** file, the **ls etc** command will be used. To get more details about the directory, like the owner, file permissions, and file size, write the **-l** after the **ls**. This **-l** command stands for long listing.

Using the Linux Help Tool

Nearly every command in Linux comes with a help file that provides guidance on how to use them. All you have to do **to** access the **help** tool is to type the name of the file alongside the **help** command. Before typing the help command, ensure to put a double dash before the word. For instance, **aircrack-ng --help.** In Linux, the convention is to use the double dash before a word and a single dash before a letter. You would notice that the **ng** letters after the **aircrack** have a single dash. This is because **ng** is not a word. Another option for accessing Linux help file, aside from the double dash before a word and the single dash before a letter, is the single dash and the question sign **-?**

Aside from the **help** command, you can also use the **manual** guide to get more details about an application. The manual guide is more detailed and more helpful than the **help** command. To access the manual, simply type **man** before the name of the application, file, or tool. For instance, to see the manual guide of the aircrack command, simply run the following command:

Kali >man aircrack-ng

This command would open the manual guide for the aircrack application. Scroll through the guide using the **Enter** key. To exit the page, type **enter q,** this would take you to the previous directory you are using before entering the manual command.

How to Find Things From the Terminals

The Linux operating system is very different from others, like Windows and Mac OS. Until you get familiar with the Linux terminal, using it can be very frustrating. However, some commands can help you master the terminal. One of these commands is **locate**.

locate

This is among the easiest commands that can help you find things from the terminal. All you have to do is type **locate** before the thing you are looking for. The command will present all the files, tools, and stuff that shares a similar description to the name you typed.

While the **locate** command can be very helpful, its result can be overwhelming. The **locate** command can present too much information such that getting the information you want would be time-consuming. Also, this command uses a database that can only be updated once in a day. This implies that you might not be able to use it more than once in a day. As a result of this, it is advisable to use the **whereis** command instead.

Using the **whereis** to find binaries

Instead of using the **locate**, if the tool you are looking for is the binaries, you can use the **whereis** command. This command displays all the necessary information about the binaries, including the source and the main page.

Using the **which** command to find the binaries

The **which** command is more specific than the **whereis** and the **locate** command. The only result it presents is the location of the binaries in the PATH variables. If the information you desire is just the location of the binaries, use the **which** command.

The **find** command

The **find** command is more detailed than the three commands explained above. It is more elaborate and flexible. With the **find** command, you would get to know the size of the tool, the date it was created, the owner of the tool, the different permissions attached to it, and the group using the tool. To use the **find** command, enter it in the following format:

kali >find /❶ -type f❷ -name apache2❸.

The command entered above is used to find the apache2. The result shows that the **find** command searches the filesystem from top to bottom. It then presents all instances of what is being looked for.

Using the **grep** command

Sometimes, while working with the command-line interface, you would want to look for a specific keyword. This action can neither be performed by the **find** command nor the **locate** command. The best command for the action is the **grep**. The **grep** helps to filter every other file and word and produce the exact keyword you are looking for. It is an effective tool for piping. Piping is the process of converting the output of a command into an input for another command. This action is carried out with the | command.

How to Modify Files and Directories

Having used one of the commands explained above to locate your file or directory, most times, you would want to modify the files. Before showing how to do this, explanations on how to create files and directories would be provided.

There are various ways to create files in Linux, and we are going to look at two of them. The first is the **cat** command, and the second is the **touch** command.

The **cat** command

Cat is a short name for **concatenate**. The command is used to join pieces of different content together. In Linux, the **cat** command is used to display the content of a file and to create smaller files with the content displayed. To use the cat command to read the content of a file, simply type cat before the file's name. To use the command to create a file, first, type cat, next, include the symbol > and the name of the file you want to create. For instance

kali >cat > hacking skills

When you type the above command and press Enter, Linux will go into the interactive mood. It would display a blank space you can use to start creating your file. When you start typing, every sentence or content would be stored in the file created. In the case of the example above, the name of the file would be **"hacking skills."** When you are done typing, and you want to exit the page, press CTRL-D. To add anything to the file when you must have

33

exited, enter the cat command with a double redirect symbol, followed by what you want to add to the file. To overwrite, enter the cat command again and a single redirect symbol.

Using the **touch command** to create a file

The **touch** command was originally designed for users to change or add details, like the date the file was created and the purpose of the file. In a situation whereby the file you want to modify does not exist, the **touch** command can be used to save the file by default.

mkdir command

When you want to create a directory in Linux, enter the **mkdir** command. For instance, if you want to create a directory named **newdirectory**, type the **mkdir** command and the name of the directory.

cp command

This command is used to copy the directory. When you enter the **cp** command, it creates a duplicate of the file and stores this in a new location. If you don't rename the new file, it will maintain the name of the old one.

Unfortunately, Linux does not have any specific commands that can be used to rename the copied file. This can only be done by using the following process:

kali >mv newfile

newfile2 kali >ls

oldfile newfile2

rm and **rmdir** commands

The **rm** command is used to remove a file while the **rmdir** command is used to remove a directory. These two commands can be used in the following pattern:

kali >rm newfile2

kali >rmdir new directory

How To Work With The User Environment Variables

In the introduction of this book, some of the important Linux tools were listed and explained. Among the tools is the shell. Shell is the interpretive environment that helps to convert the series of commands run on the Linux operating system into source code. The basic type of shell used by Linux is the bash. This section provides more explanation of the shell and the user environment.

In Linux, there are two major types of variables. These include the shell and the environment. Before explaining these variables, it is important to understand what variables mean. Variable is a term used to refer to strings in key=value. A variable can be just one string or multiple strings. In the case of Linux, there are multiple types of strings. Hence we have KEY = value1:value2 etc.

On the one hand, the environment variables are responsible for the outlook of the Linux operating system. As well as controlling the action of the system, environment variables are system-wide variables and are inherited by any child shell. The default environment in Kali Linux is the bash shell. When using the Kali Linux, each user has its own default environment variables. The variables can be adjusted to make the system work effectively. It can also be modified to affect the look and action of the environment. Environment variables are usually written in upper case, such as PATH, HOME, and SHELL. On the other hand, the shell variables can only be used in the shell they are listed in. They are typically listed in lowercase.

To view your default environment, enter the **env** command into the terminal using any directory of your choice. However, viewing the environment variables is a little different. Environment variables include the local variables, shell variables, shell functions, like the command aliases, and the user-defined variables. To view these variables, use the **set** command. This command will present a detailed list of all the environment variables applicable to your system. The output list can be so long that you would need to keep scrolling down to view them. To make viewing the variables less stressful, you can use the **set** command and then pipe it into the **more** command. This action would present the list of the variables line by line.

Although the process of viewing the variables can be made less stressful by the **set** and **more** command, this action can be further managed by filtering through the result. To do this, use the **grep** command. The **grep** command allows you to view the particular variable you are interested in.

How to Change the Variable Value

In the above explanation of the variable, it was mentioned that the value of the environment variable could be changed to make the system work effectively. To change the value of the variable, pipe the **set** command with **grep** to locate the specific variable you want to change. Set the present value of your variable to any digit of your choice. When you do this, the system will not save any of your past commands. However, the changes you made would only be temporary. It occurs only in the variable environment. Thus, when you close the terminal, the changes return back to the previous value.

To change your variable value permanently, use the export command. This command will transfer the new value from the variable environment to the rest of the system. The new variable value will be available in all the environment until it is changed.

Note: variables are strings; as such, it is advisable to save the value of the variable in a different file before changing it.

How to change the shell prompt.

Shell prompt is one of the environment variables that exist in Linux Kali. This variable provides vital information like the directory and the user operating system that is currently being used. Kali default shell prompt takes the following format:

username@hostname:current_directory

If the user operating system you are using is the root, the format would be:

root@kali:current_directory

To change the name of the default shell prompt, set the value of the PS1 variable. This variable contains information such as:

\h   The hostname

\u   The name of the current user

\w The basename of the current directory.

Setting the value of the PS1 variable is important if you are using the multiple shells on the system. This enables you to recognize the user and name at a glance. An example of a change PSI variable is:

kali >PS1="World's Best Hacker: #"

For this setting, any time you use the terminal, you would be reminded that you are the "world's best hacker." However, this setting only applies to the terminal session. Any other terminal you opened would still have the default command prompt.

How to Change Your Path

The path variable is one of the most important variables in the environment variable. It controls where the shell would look for the commands entered on the system. Usually, commands are stored in the sbin or bin subdirectory, such as the /usr/local/sbin or usr/local/bin. If during the process of looking for the command, the bash shell is unable to locate the file in any of the directories in the PATH, it would return the error as *command not found*, even if the command is stored in other directories not present in the PATH. To find the directories that are stored in the PATH, use the **echo** command. However, while typing this command, ensure to add $ symbol to the PATH. Your program should be in this format:

kali >echo $PATH

/usr/local/sbin:usr/local/bin:/usr/sbin:/sbin/bin

Adding Directories to the PATH Variables

This exercise is important because it makes it easy to access the variables in the PATH. For instance, when a new tool is downloaded into a different directory like the /root/newhackingtool. Since this tool is not saved into the PATH variable, accessing the file would require that you first navigate to /root/newhackingtool. To save yourself from this stress, save the tool into the PATH variable by entering the following command:

kali >PATH=$PATH:/root/newhackingtool

This action allows you to execute the application from any part of the system.

How to Create a User-Defined Variable

The simplest way to create a user-defined variable is to add a new value to a variable you have already named. This process is very useful if you are working with a long command or writing more advanced shell scripting. To create a user-defined variable, first enter the name of the variable, followed by the equal sign (=), and then the value you want to put in the variable. The action should be similar to this:

> kali >MYNEWVARIABLE="Hacking is the most valuable skill set in the 21st century."

To see the value of the new variable, enter the echo command, followed by the name of the variable. However, there should be a $ sign before the name of the variable. This process would be in this pattern:

> kali >echo $MYNEWVARIABLE

Hacking is the most valuable skill set in the 21st century.

To delete this variable, use the **unset** command.

Chapter Four

Building A Kali Website Server

A server is a computer program that necessitates functionality for diverse programs. Servers perform various services, such as executing computation for clients or sharing data among several clients. One server can be useful for several clients, and one client can use several servers. The necessary servers are:

- Database servers,

- Mail servers,

- print servers,

- Game servers,

- Application servers,

- File servers,

- And web servers.

Our focus for now is the web server.

Having defined what a server is, we shall unravel the importance of a web server. However, it is important to know some things about sockets before building a web server. A socket is the delineation of internal endpoints that are meant for sending and receiving information within a node.

Sockets are essentially entities that connect a communication channel between two processes or programs. This process could be referred to as network communication. These communications cannot function properly without sockets. A socket is created when we open any website in our server, which connects to the distant web server. The web server receives the connection and sends us the web page we have demanded.

Internet socket, also known as INET socket, is IP protocol based. Sockets may have basis meanings based on the context. A *client* socket is an endpoint of interaction while a *server* socket operates like a switchboard operator. Your browser is an example of client programming. Therefore, it uses the client socket. However, the web server uses both the client and the server sockets.

To create a web server, the file will run through the terminal, which stimulates the server to run a Python script. Study the guidelines below:

- Type Python, after which you will write the name of the file. The socket has been created at this point, and it has been put to listening mode. Connect to this server through another terminal called the *telnet* command. You can choose any port if you do not want to use the common *8080*. The port numbers are from 0 to 65535, but 0 to 1023 are set aside.

There are now two terminals: the first runs your Python file while the second runs your newly designed Kali web server on port 8080.

- Observe the second terminal. Telnet command would now connect to the newly created server. As soon as it gets connected, the first terminal will display this output:

pg@kali:-/pyCharmProjects/KaliServer$ Python myserver.py

At this point, your Kali Linux web server has been created.

For additional penetration testing, install PyCharm and the Wing IDE Editor to create more Python Code. PyCharm is free, and it has wider features, which makes it preferable to the Wing IDE Editor. There are basically the versions of the Wing, namely the Wing professional version and the Wing personal version. The Wing professional version has a complete featured Python IDE. In contrast, the Wing personal version has a free Python IDE for a person interested in a particular subject or students. For the PyCharm also, the professional version is a complete featured IDE for Python and web development. In contrast, the community version is free and has a little ability IDE for Python and scientific growth.

It is very easy to install PyCharm through the Wing Python editor. To install it through the terminal, type this command: *sudo apt-get install PyCharm- community.*

For penetration testing, an ethical hacker needs to stay anonymous because they have to use their Kali Linux server repeatedly. There are some tricks to know in order for the ethical hacker to become anonymous. One of these tricks is to use the Tor browser.

The first step to take is to install the Tor browser. It can be downloaded from *https://torproject.org.* Tor preserves your anonymity through multiple proxies. Kali Linux also provides a unique privilege to modify the configuration at the root to ensure that you can hide your real identity using Tor for browsing the web.

To configure your proxy chains.conf file, open the configuration file using the leaf pad text editor and then open your Kali Linux terminal as a root user and type in this command:*su leafpad/etc/ proxychains.conf.*

The proxychains.conf file will open. You can use different types of proxies, but not at the same time. It is better to use the Dynamic chain so that if one proxy fails, the other one will pickup

Another significant concept to be considered is a virtual private network (VPN). However, an important segment to be familiar with is the DNS system. It is through DNS that your Internet Protocol(IP) address is hidden using a VPN. To start using the VPN, download it from www.vpnbook.com. A combination of username and password is given when downloading it. Save them because you will need them to run the virtual private network on your system. Unzip the zipped version of the VPN you have downloaded using this command: root@kali:-/Downloads#unzip VPNBook.com-Open VPN-DE1.zip.

While downloading the openvpn zipped folder, write down your username and password in a separate text file. You will need them to run the previous code.

Virtual Machines

Virtual is a technological device that can be used to run different operating systems from single hardware. The hardware could be a laptop or a desktop. Mastering how to use this device is important because, with a virtual machine, you can run your Window or MacOS operating system alongside the Kali Linux. This implies that when using the Virtual Machine, you won't need a different operating system.

There are different types of virtual machine applications that can be gotten from applications such as Oracle, VMware, and Microsoft. While all of these are very good, the one that would be explained is the Oracle. Oracle can be freely downloaded from *VirtualBox*

How to Install VirtualBox

To download the VirtualBox, go to https://www.virtualbox.org/. The **Download** button would reflect at the left menu, click on this and select the VirtualBox package that suites the current operating system you are using. Your operating system would store the VirtualBox VM you downloaded.

When you are through with the download, proceed to the setup file, click on it. When you do, a setup Wizard will display. Click on the **Next** menu below the screen. This would redirect you to the custom setup screen. Next, click on the **Next** menu below the screen. Continue to click on next until you get to the **Network Interface**. When you do, click on **Yes**.

Having downloaded the VirtualBox, the next thing to do is to install it. To start this process, click on **Install**. While the installation is going on, you would be constantly notified to install device software. Ensure you install all the device software that is displayed. This is necessary because they are important for the effectiveness of your virtual machine. Without the device software, your virtual machine might not be able to communicate.

Note: when downloading the VirtualBox, ensure it is the latest version.

How to Set Up Your Virtual Machine

After you have successfully downloaded and installed your virtual machine, click on open. When you do, the virtual machine manager will pop up. Since the virtual machine we are downloading would be working with the Kali Linux, go to the upper-right corner and click on **New**. This redirects you to the Create Virtual Machine dialog, where you will find three spaces to fill in this page. The first is the **Name** column. Here you would be required to give your machine a name. The second is the **Type**, simply fill in **Linux** in this column. The last column is the **Version**, select **Debian (64bit)** to fill this column. After completing the three options, click on **Next.** The new page would require that you select the quantity of RAM you would allocate to your virtual machine. It is advisable that when allocating, do not let your RAM space for your VM be more than 25 percent of your total RAM space.

Therefore, assuming your system's total RAM space is 16Gb, do not allocate more than 4Gb to your virtual machine. If it is 4Gb, do not allocate more than 1Gb. The reason for this is because your current operating system needs more space than your virtual machine. Also, other applications on your device would need space. However, your virtual machine would not consume any RAM space unless it is being used. The only space it would take would be on the hard drive.

After allocating your virtual machine's RAM space, click on **Next.** This would take you to the Hard Disk page. Click **Create Virtual Hard Disk**. Next, click **Create**. After this, a page similar to the allocates space page would poop up. However, on this page, you would be required to choose between dynamic hard drive space or fixed space. The best option between the two is **Dynamically Allocated.** In this option, the virtual drive would not take the entire space allocated to it unless it needs it. This helps to save more hard drive space for your operating system. When you have chosen the dynamically allocated, click Next and choose the amount of space you want to allocate to the virtual machine. To be on the safe side, it is advisable to choose a high size of space between 15 and 25GB. This is because when you allocate a smaller space, as you continue to use your virtual machine, it can run out of space. When it does, expanding your hard drive space can be very risky. After choosing your space capacity, click Create.

How to Install Kali on Your Virtual Machine

At this point, the page on your screen would be "welcome to virtualbox." However, on the left side of the VirtualBox manager, you would notice that the Kali VM is off. This is because you are yet to install Kali on your virtual box, to do this, click on the **Start** menu. Next, the VirtualBox manager would ask you where the startup disk is located. By now, you should have the disk image with the extension. iso in your download folder. The only exception to this is if you use a torrent to download your Kali. If you do, the **.iso** file will be stored in the **iso** folder in the torrenting application. When you locate the folder, click on it, and select the Kali image. Next, click **Start**. Your Kali has been successfully installed into your VirtualBox. The next action is to set up the Kali.

How to Set Up the Kali

When you have successfully installed the Kali, the page on your screen would be the Kali page. On the page, there would be a lot of startup choices to use. Among these numerous choices, it is advisable to use the graphical install.

However, if you encounter any error while installing Kali into your VirtualBox, you might not be redirected to this page. The reason for the error is often because your system BIOS is not virtualization enabled. The BIOS for every system is slightly different; as a result, this can only be solved by the manufacturer. The solution for most systems can be gotten online. In addition to this, you would need to disable any competing virtualization software on your Windows system. A good example of such software is Hyper-V.

If you successfully install Kali and have clicked on the graphical install, you would be asked to choose a language. Ensure that you choose a language you can work comfortably with. After this, click on **continue**, select your **location,** and click on **continue** again. Next, choose your keyboard layout and click on continue. When you complete these processes, VirtualBox will take some time to detect your network adapters and your hardware. After successful detection, the next stage is to configure your network.

In the network configuring stage, the first option is to choose a name for your host. Choose any name of your choice and proceed to the next option. Here you would be asked to fill a domain name. This aspect is not as important as the first one; hence it can be left blank. Click on **continue**. The next option is the password. This is very important and must be filled with a strong password. The password you filled is what you will use to access the root user.

In Linux, the root user is a very powerful system administrator. Therefore, your password should be a very complex one that would be difficult to guess by hackers. Having chosen the password, click on Continue. The next option is to set a time zone, do this, and click continue. The next option would ask you for a partition disk. This simply means a portion of your hard drive. Select Guided - use the entire disk. When you do, Kali would first detect your hard drive and fix the partition disk automatically. Next, a warning would pop up that all data in the disk would be erased since the virtual disk is still new and empty, there is nothing to worry about. Click on continue. Kali would ask if you want your files in a separate partition or, in one partition, click on **all files in one partition.** Next, click on Finish Partitioning and write changes to disk to write your changes to disk. When you do, click Yes and Continue. When you finish this process, Kali will start installing the operating system of your device. This would take a while to complete.

Once the installation is completed, you would be asked if you want to use the network mirror. This option is of little or no importance; hence it is better to choose **no**. Next, kali would ask you if you want to install the GRUB (Grand Unified Bootloader). Click on Yes and continue. The GRUB allows you to change your operating system from Kali to any other one of your choice. The next option is to choose between installing the GRUB manually or automatically. Choose manual installation. This is because most times, automatic installation tends to hang and might not be successful. When you choose the manual installation, choose the drive where you want the GRUB to be installed to and click on next. You have successfully installed your Kali.

Click on Continue to reboot your Kali. Next, log in as root and enter the password you used for your root user. When your login is successful, you can start using your Kali Linux Desktop.

How to Map the Wireless Adapter Into Your Kali

This stage is very important if you are using an external wireless USB adapter with your kali. To connect the USB to the Linux Kali, go to the VirtualBox menu. Next, navigate to the Device|USB and choose the right USB device. This simple action would connect the USB directly to the Kali Linux. You can access the Kali Device with the GUI tool or the command line. To check if the wireless adapter is working effectively and supported by the modes running on the system, open a terminal window and run the following commands:

lsusb

iwconfig

- Isusb

This command helps you to see if the USB is connected to the system. If the USB is connected, create a short description of the device for easy identification. This command lists out all the devices connected to the system.

- iwconfig

This command is used to view and set the mode of the wireless interface. It allows you to see the mode the interface is working in. With this command, you would be able to bring the interface up and down.

Having ensured that the wireless device is working well with the Kali operating system, verify if all the modes of the system are supported by the wireless device. To carry out this action, run the **iw** command in Kali.

In Kali, **iw** command is used to show and manipulate the configuration of the wireless devices. During the process of the command, it would redirect you to the **phy** option. This option tells the command to use its physical address to select the interface. This action is followed by the physical address identifier. After which, the **trailing** option directs the **iw** command to print all the details of the connected wireless device.

When the command presents the details of all the wireless devices, to identify the interface you need, you would need to scroll up. Another important command to run is the **iwlist**. This command allows the wireless device to validate all the connected mode in preparation for the penetration test. With the **iwlist**, you can access other details not presented by the **iw** command. These would include the key in use, encryption capabilities, power level, and transmission rate.

Chapter Five

Network Management

$$\Longrightarrow\!\!\!\!-\!\!\!\!(\!(\!\!\!\!-\!\!\!\!\!\bullet\!\!\!\!\!-\!\!\!\!\!)\!)\!\!\!\!-\!\!\!\!\Longleftarrow$$

In-depth knowledge of networking is very crucial to anyone who wants to become a professional hacker. Since you will be dealing mostly with the network, you must understand how to connect to and operate the network. The tools for managing networks during hacking will be discussed in this chapter.

Network security is highly important to ethical hacking because security has to first start from the network. Ethical hackers need to understand the different layers in which data travels. Once they can understand how networking operates, they can easily trace or retrieve data. To operate a wireless network on your desktop, you will need to buy a different wireless network adapter that you will plug into the computer's USB port. Still, for laptops, the wireless adapter is inbuilt. You need a switch to connect many computers with a network cable. It is this switch that controls the sharing.

Three things are essential in networking, and they are files, resources, and applications.

Networking has to do with different computers and devices connected together to process and share data or information.

The network operates through devices such as computers, routers, switches, servers, and so on. These devices comprise services and resources. They provide services such as switching, routing, data transmission, and so on.

The primary function of networking is to connect users together so that they can see these services, and its second function is to organize a system such that the devices permit the users to share information or resources effectively.

When networking began, it was observed that the software and the hardware could not work effectively together. It became a serious challenge. To create a solution to this, a mutual network design with a communication operator is needed. This will enable different devices to interact with one another. This brought about what is referred to as internetworking models. There are basically two types of internetworking models, namely the open Systems interconnections (OSI) reference model, and the transmission control protocol or Internet protocol model.

The Open Systems Interconnections (OSI)

The OSI reference model was created by the International Organization for Standardization (IOS). This model has seven layers which are:

- Application (7)

- Presentation (6)

- Session (5)

- Transport (4)

- Network (3)

- Datalink (2)

- Physical (1)

We need to understand how these layers are interconnected. Assuming a user wants to open a web page, the first thing he does is to send a request to the server that is far away from him. The server's hard disk is the first layer, which is physical. The user's first request is the application layer, which is the seventh layer and then proceeds to the sixth layer, which is the presentation layer. Note that the application layer primarily handles the user's interaction through his device, which could be a phone or a computer. Data is formatted in the sixth layer and then moves to the fifth layer, which is the session layer. The scene enters in this layer and controls the end to end interaction. Up to the fifth layer, the name of what is being transmitted is data. However, when it enters the fourth layer, which is transport, its name changes to *segment.* It is called segment in this layer because it breaks your request into various components. It includes the origin and destination port numbers and makes it secure by adding serial numbers. Then, your request journeys down to the third layer, which is the network layer; it is now referred to as a packet. It is in this layer that IP addresses are added to the origin and destination of your request. It also enables it to find the right route to its destination. Your data request will now proceed to the second layer, which is the data link layer. This layer adds origin and destination MAC addresses and then goes through the Frame Check System (FCS) processes. It examines whether the request has reached its final destination, which is the first layer, the physical layer. It is now referred to as bits and bytes. The physical layer could be laptops, desktops, printers, and servers.

This model comes with four layers. They are:

The Transmission Control Protocol

- Application

- Transport

- Internet

- Network Access

These layers are similar to the ones in the OSI model. The sessions and the presentations of the OSI model are similar to the Application layer of TCP. The Network Access layer is similar to the physical layer in the OSI model. The internet layer of TCP is similar to the Network layer in the OSI model. The Transport layer of TCP is similar to the Transport layer in the OSI model

One of the most effective tools for examining and operating with practical network interfaces is the IFCONFIG command. IFCONFIG will show some important information about the active network interfaces on the computer. The name of the first discovered interface at the top of the output is Etherneto, which is shortened as eth0 (1). More other Etherneto interfaces will show up as eth1, eth2, eth3, eth4 on, and on like that. The next thing that will show is the type of network being used, which is Etherneto and a globally special address stamped on all network hardware or the Media Access Control (MAC) address. The next process is the broadcast address shortened as the Bcast. This is needed for sending Information to all the IPs on the subnet. The final process is the network mask, which is needed to ascertain what segment of the IP address is connected to the local network.

Another section of the output is a loopback address. It is also referred to as localhost. It is a unique software address that links you to your own computer, and only software or services running on your computer can use it. The loopback or localhost is widely presented with the IP address as 127.0.0.1.

IFCONFIG helps the hacker to connect to and control the local area network (LAN) settings.

To check wireless network devices, IWCONFIG command is needed. This command can be used to gather essential information for wireless hacking, like the IP address, what mode it is in, and the MAC address and so on. The information you get from this command is vital, especially when you are using a wireless hacking tool such as aircrack-ng. The terminal is also used to access this command.

Another important trick you should have as a hacker or a prospecting hacker is being able to change your network information or your IP address in order to enable you to access other networks while appearing as a reliable device on those networks. Changing your IP address is very simple and straightforward. All you need to do is to enter ifconfig and then the interface you want to redesignate with the new IP address. When this is done properly, Linux will just return the command reminder. When you go back to your ifconfig connection, your IP address should have changed to the new IP address you have designated.

Furthermore, you can use the IFCONFIG command to change your Media Access Control (MAC) address. This address is significant in the sense that it is frequently used as a security measure to restrain hackers from networks. To send up your MAC address, use the down option of the ifconfig command, enter the ifconfig command and the interface name followed by the new MAC address. Note that the interface could be hardware, shortened as *hw* or Ethernet, shortened as *ether.* Then, finally, bring the interface up with the *up* option to effect the change. By the time you check your ifconfig settings, your new MAC address should have reflected on it.

Another interesting trick Linux helps to achieve is designating new IP addresses from the Dynamic Host Configuration Protocol (DHCP) server. What the DHCP server does is to designate IP addresses to all the systems on the subnet and protect log files in which the IP address is set aside to a device. It is very useful for forensic hacking to trace fraudsters after an attack.

The Domain Name And IP Address

The domain name system (DNS) is one of the effective places hackers can access vital information. DNS is a critical aspect of the internet and often used to translate domain names to IP addresses. When the DNS is used to translate a domain name to an IP address, the result makes it easy for the system to work on. Without the domain name, remembering all the IP addresses we want to execute would be a very difficult task.

One of the most useful tools hackers can use to gather DNS information is the **dig** command. The dig command enables the haver to access stored information about a domain. This information might include a target IP address and email. An example of dig command execution is **kali >dig hackers-arise.com ns.** This command would display three sections: the question, answer, and additional sections. The additional section would contain the IP address of the domain name.

dig command can also be used to get information on an email server connected to the domain name. To get this information, you would add the **mx** option to the dig command. If you need information on the attack on email, it is important to run this command.

The most common DNS in Linux is the Berkeley Internet Name Domain (BIND)

In a situation whereby you want to use another DNS server, you will have to open a plain text on the text editor and edit it. After this, go to your command line and enter the name of the editor. Next, enter the name of the file and the location of the file. You have successfully changed your DNS server.

Aside from the **dig** command, you can also use a special file called the **host** file to translate the domain name into an IP address. With the **host** file, you can specify your own IP address. This added advantage can be used to hijack a TCP connection on your local area network.

However, it is important to note that to use the host file, you would need to master tools like the **dnsspoof** and **Ettercap**. With a good mastery of these tools, you will be able to use the host file to direct traffics on your LAN.

Chapter Six

File Manipulation

W ith Linux, frequent commands can be learned easily. Test files are paramount to Linux. As a result of many text files, controlling texts becomes essential in managing Linux programs. For you to become a prominent ethical hacker, you have to be familiar with elementary Kali Linux terminals and commands such as Metasploit or Nmap, as well as mastering Linux programming. Linux commands will not only inform you about the system itself but also inform you of where the file system is located or where you are on the system. Also, you will be informed on how to modify the permission of a file system.

To search for the Kali terminal, ensure you have first of all installed Kali Linux. Find the applications link on the top left of your screen and click on it to open a list of applications. You will see a default browser of Kali called *Iceweasel* on top of the list. It will not leave you anonymous because it is an extension of the usual Mozilla Firefox. After this, you will see the command-line tool, otherwise called the terminal. This tool will be needed since it deals with all kinds of keyboard inputs. Next to the command-line tool is the *Files* folder,, and the next thing you will observe are the hacking devices such as Burp Suite, Armitage, Metasploit, etc.

After opening the command tool, you can either maximize it or minimize it. To maximize it, press Ctrl+Shift and then press the + sign, to minimize it, press Ctrl+Shift and press the - sign

Another trick used frequently in Linux is working with text files. **To** write a text file quickly, you can use nano, which is also from Linux distribution. To achieve this, follow the guidelines below:

- Type nano in your terminal. It will open up a text editor on the terminal.

- Enter this command in your terminal: *nano novel.txt*. Nano will open the file after entering the command.

- Edit any part by pressing Ctrl+O and saving it.

- Exit the file by pressing Ctrl+X

- To read the new file with your cat command, issue a command on your terminal this way: cat novel.txt.

To show just part of a text file, use the *head,* and the *tail* commands. The *head* is used to view just the beginning of a file. This command, by design, shows the first ten lines of a text file. The *tail* is used to view the lady ten lines of a text file. The following command produces the first ten lines: kali> ***head/etc/snort/snort.conf.*** However, if you wish to see fewer or more lines than the first ten designed lines, add the quantity you want with the dash(-). Type it this way:

kali> ***head -30/etc/snort/snort. conf.*** To view the last ten lines of the text file, type: Kali> ***tail/etc/snort/snort. conf.*** However, to view more than ten lines or any quantity, add the quantity and the dash (-) to the command:

Kali> ***tail -30/etc/snort/snort. conf.***

Furthermore, numbering the lines will be very helpful because *snort.conf* has over six hundred lines. If you number the lines, it will be very easy for you to make references while modifying any part of the file. In other words, it allows you to go back to a particular location within the file without getting confused. To add numbers to the lines, enter this command:

Kali>**nl/etc/snort/snort.com.**

The most commonly used file manipulation command is *grep*. It allows you to separate unwanted elements from the content of a file for display. For example, if you want to view all the lines that have the word *article* in your file, type and enter this command:

Kali>**cat/etc/snort/snort.conf/grep article**

Only the lines that have the word *article* will be displayed. The *grep* command is such an effective tool that will save you the stress of searching for all the lines where the word occurs because it could be time-consuming and energy-sapping.

To find and replace, just like in Windows, the se*e command* is potent in helping you achieve this. *Sed* is a contraction of *stream* *editor* since it performs the same function as a stream editor. It helps you to find a word as well as replace it with another word of your choice. For instance, if you want *sed* to replace every occurrence of the word *leave* with the word *exit,* as well as save the file with *conf*, type and enter this command:

Kali> **sed s /leave/exit/g/etc/snort/snort.conf> conf**

The *s* command searches for every occurrence of the word *leave* while the *g* command informs Linux that the replacement should reflect globally. You can as well use the *sed* commands to replace a specific occurrence of a word rather than the entire occurrences of the word. If, for example, you want to replace only the fourth occurrence of the word *leave* and replace it with *exit*, just place the number of the occurrence at the end of the command:

Kali> **sed s/leave/exit/4 snort.conf> conf.**

When displaying large files, *cat* could be the wrong command to use because it can only display and create small files. To work with larger files, there are two effective commands which are: *more* and *less.*

The *more* command unfurls a file page at once and allows you to scroll down through it using the ENTER key. Type this command to achieve this, type and enter:

Kali>**more/etc/snort/snort.conf.**

The *less* command has an added function than the *more* command. You can scroll through a file with *less* command as well as filter it for words. Type this command:

Kali> **less/etc/snort/snort.conf.**

Chapter Seven

Scrutinizing Wireless Networks
And Scanning

To become a professional hacker, you must have the ability to connect to network devices from your computer. You can have access to private information on a device if you can hack a wireless connection. We will be focusing on the two prominent wireless technologies, namely: Bluetooth and Wi-Fi.

Bluetooth Connection

To hack or exploit Bluetooth, you need to have an in-depth knowledge of how it works. Bluetooth was developed by Ericsson Corp of Sweden in 1994 and named after Danish King Harald Bluetooth, who lived in the 10th century. In recent days, almost all the devices and systems have Bluetooth as a non-detachable part of their functionality. Examples of such devices are smartphones, tablets, keyboards, iPods, speakers, and so on.

When two Bluetooth devices are connected, it is referred to as *pairing*. However, they have to be in discoverable mode before they can connect. Through Bluetooth, names, technical information, and a list of services can be released. When the two devices are connected together via Bluetooth, they exchange a private or link key. Each device stores this link key **to** identify the other when paired together. To scan for Bluetooth signals, Linux has a tool of the Bluetooth policy stack known as BlueZ. Some Linux distributions have it already installed but if it is not, in yours, you can install it using this command: *Kali>**apt-get install bluez.***

There are some simple tools Bluez has, for the purpose of scanning and managing Bluetooth devices. They are *hciconfig, hcitool, hcidump,* and *sdptool.* Each of them are see refined below:

hciconfig: This is a tool that performs almost the same function as ***ifconfig*** in Linux. The first step to take while scanning with Bluetooth is to determine if the Bluetooth adapter on the system being used is acknowledged and capable of using so that it can be used to scan for over devices. Once the Bluetooth adapter is acknowledged with a MAC address, you can proceed to check if the connection is capable of using. Provide the name and the *up* command: *Kali>**hciconfig hci0 up***. A prompt will pop on the screen to indicate whether it is successful or not.

hcitool is another BlueZ tool that investigates and supplies us with information such as the device name, device class, clock information, and device identity. This information enables connected devices to function together simultaneously. It is used to scan for other Bluetooth devices within that area. To scan for Bluetooth devices in discovery mode, type this: *Kali>**hcitool inq.*** You will now see information, such as the MAC addresses of both devices, the class of both devices, and the clock information

67

displayed. To get more information about the functions of **hcitool,** go to the help page by typing: Kali>**hcitool --help.** You will find the usage and commands which enable scanning for remote devices, finding names from remote devices, displaying local devices, and investigating remote devices.

Sdptool is also a BlueZ tool that browses for the function it provides. However, the device does not have to be in discovery mode, like the **hcitool,** before it can be scanned. To scan using this tool, type in this format: sdptool browse MAC address.

Wi-Fi Network

To understand Wi-Fi Network, we need to be familiar with its operations. Wi-Fi can function in any of its 14 channels. For access to the internet, wireless users connect to the access point (AP) device; the nearer you are to the Wi-Fi AP, the higher the power, and the smoother the connection clicks. Wi-Fi is structured to function on 2.4GHz and 5GHz. If you are confused with which Wi-Fi access points you should connect to, check for wireless access points your network card can deliver by using the *iwlist* command. Type it in this format: iwlist *interface action.* You can use this action to scan all the Wi-Fi access points in your area. This command should provide you :

- All Wi-Fi access points within the area of your wireless interface

- The MAC address of the AP

- The frequency

- The channel it is operating on

- Its signal level

- Its quality

- Its extended service set identifier

and to determine if the encryption key is enabled.

Furthermore, Wi-Fi can function in any of these three modes: master, managed, and monitor. *Master* implies that it is set to act as an AP; *managed* implies it is set to connect with an AP or has connected with an AP; *monitor* enables wireless network cards to detect all the traffic passing its path.

Another helpful command you can use in managing your Wi-Fi connections is *nmcli.* You can use this tool to access the Wi-Fi APs close to you. To use it, type in this format: *nmcli devices network type.* Since we are dealing with Wi-Fi, the network type will be *Wifi.* In a more precise way, type: Kali> ***nmci dev wifi.***

To gain access to a Wi-Fi AP, you must know the MAC address or the basic service set identifier, the channel the AP operates on, and the MAC address of the client. All this information can be gotten from the aircrack-ng suite. This suite is available in all versions of Linux Kali; hence there is no need to download another one.

To use the tool effectively, you would need first to set your wireless network card into monitor mode. This mode allows the network to see all the traffic passing its way. Usually, a network card that is not set into the monitor mode cannot see beyond the traffics designed for the card alone. This is why monitor mode is often referred to as promiscuous mode.

To set your wireless network card into monitor mode, go to the aircrack-ng suite and use the airmon-ng command. The command should be in this format: kali >airmon-ng start wlan0. To stop or restart the monitor mode, use the **stop or restart command.**

It is important to note that when you set your network card into monitor mode, the airmon-ng would change the name of your wireless interface. Ensure you take note of the new name because you would need it in the next action.

The next action is how to use other tools from the aircrack-ng suite to search for key data from the wireless traffic. The first tool to examine is the airodump-ng command. This command is used to capture and display the key data from broadcasting APs, and every client connected to the APs. To use the airodump-ng, plug in the airodump-ng, and then input the interface name you got from the airmong-ng. Once this command is issued, the wireless card gathers all the vital information from the wireless traffic of all nearby APs.

However, you would notice that the information gathered by the wireless card is displayed in a split-screen format. There is the upper portion and the lower portion. The reason for this is because the information gathered is in two vital forms. The upper portion is made up of information about the broadcasting APs. This includes:

- The power of the APs

- The BSSID

- The number of beacon frames that are detected

- The number of package data that have traversed the wireless card

- The data throughput rate

- The theoretical throughput limit

- The channel

- The encryption protocol

- Authentication type

- The cipher used for authentication

- The ESSID or SSID.

The lower portion is made up of the client access information. This includes the number of clients that are not associated. These types of clients are those detected in the process of gathering information from the wireless network, but not connected to any AP. The next type of clients are those associated with a station; this implies that they are connected to the AP.

These are the information needed to crack the AP. However, to crack the wireless AP, you would need the AP MAC address, the client MAC address, a password list, and the channel the target is operating on.

The next action is cracking a Wi-Fi password. However, to do this, you would need to open three terminals. The first terminal includes filling in the client, the channel, and the AP MAC addresses. The second terminal includes using the aireplay-ng command to deauthenticate anyone connected to the AP. This action forces the clients to reauthenticate; during this process, you can easily capture the hash of their password. The password hash would be displayed in the upper right corner of the airodump-ng terminal. The last terminal includes using the password list to find out the password of the hashes that were captured.

Wireless command with wifi

In Linux, the basic wireless command used in listing every activated network interface on the system is ifconfig. Also, the ifconfig command is used in listing the IP address of every interface on the system and some basic statistics. When the ifconfig command is run, the wifi interface would be provided as wlanX. This result is the designated Wi-Fi interface in Kali Linux. X stands for the number of the interface. Hence, when the ifconfig command is run, the first Wi-Fi interface would be shown as wlano, the second as wlan1, and the third as wlan2.

To see the specific Wi-Fi interface and their numbers, use the **iwconfig** command.

Scanning

The scanning phase is the initial stage of the pen-testing. Before beginning the pen-testing, scanning must first be done. This is because the output of the scanning phase is used to determine how the pen test will be run. The results of the scanning phase include the current access point of the system and the clients operating environment. Scanning can be carried out on the phone, laptops, and every other device capable of running a wireless sniffing. However, since the concentration of this book is Linux Kali, the tools that would be examined are those available in Linux Kali.

The wireless scanning tools in Kali include kismet or airodump-ng. The tools can be connected to interfaces and placed on monitor mode. While in this mode, the tool travels through the wireless spectrum across the system and gathers wireless packets. The result of the scan can either be displayed on the screen or saved in a file. To analyze this result, you can use either the airgraph-ng tool in generating a visual graph or carry out a manual analysis. Once the scanning phase has been completed and the output has been analyzed, the result would be used in pen-testing.

The result of the analysis can be used in pen-testing to remove unauthorized clients and access points. It can also be used to prioritize clients and networks in order of their importance to the pentest. However, it is important to note that the airodump-ng is not the only scanning tool in Kali; the Raspberry Pi can also be used to carry out this action. Before explaining how this tool can be used, an explanation of the two major types of scanning will be provided. These include:

- Active scanning

- Passive scanning

Passive Scanning

Generally, there are two ways the access point can be discovered. It can be discovered either by a passive scan or an active scan. What determines the method that would be used is the configuration of the client station. In passive scanning, the client station searches for the beacon frame from the access point. During this process, it also searches out all the SSIDs in the network. When it discovers any SSID, it tries to initiate a connection. If the SSID is more than one, the client station chooses the AP with the best signal. The passive scanning is different from the active scanning because the client station does not engage in an active search. As a result, it will not be able to search out non-beaconing APs.

In most systems, the network system administrator turns off the default system APs. This is a precautionary measure used to avoid detection. When using the passive scanning in this kind of situation, the client station might not be able to detect the WLAN.

Active Scanning

In passive scanning, it was explained that the client searches for a beacon frame from the access point, while, in active scanning, the client station sends probe request frames with the SSID field set to a null or preferred SSID. When the probe is sent, the access points listen to this and reply with the probe response frame. This frame contains all the data available in the beacon frame. With this method, all non-beaconing frames also respond to the probe and reveal their presence. Therefore, the active scanning produces results containing the beacon frame and non-beacon frame. The result is more in-depth than passive scanning.

However, there are situations whereby the network administrator would configure the access points to ignore all probes. This can be removed by configuring the client station with a valid SSID.

Chapter Eight

Process Creation and Management

A process is a program that is executing. It could also be defined as a task that is running and employing other resources. Operating a process includes a web server, a terminal, running commands, GUI interface, databases, and so on. To be a professional hacker, using Linux commands, you need to understand how to control your processes and make your computer programming more efficient. A hacker may have a target program that needs to stop **to** find another process. Also, the hacker may need to set a schedule running periodically. This chapter will help you discover how you can run processes in the background, prioritize them, and stop them if necessary. We will start with how to view processes and then move on to how they can be managed or controlled.

One of the Linux commands used to view processes is the *ps* command. Subsequently, the Linux Kernel, which controls virtually everything, designates a special process called *process ID* to each process as they are being created. You need to state their process ID explicitly when operating with these processes in Linux. When the ps command is functioning without other options, it outlines the processes started by the current user and the processes functioning on that terminal. However, if we need more information, especially on processes run by other users, as well as what is going on in the background, we need to run the ps command with the options *aux*. Ensure you do not use uppercase in typing your command because Linux is case sensitive. Type in lowercase: kali> ***ps aux.*** This will enable you to get the desired result.

When there is too much information displayed on the screen, the user may get confused, trying to operate everything at once. To avoid processes displaying on the screen, use the grep command. Processes are ordered by a process ID number, and they are displayed in the order that the user started them.

The Metasploit exploitation structure is the most commonly employed exploitation structure used to demonstrate. This tool is mostly used by professional hackers, and it is usually installed on the Kali system. To use this tool, type: Kali > ***msfconsole***. To determine if the exploitation processes have started, enter the following command: Kali> **ps aux/grep msfconsole**

We may want to know which process is using the most resources. To achieve this, we need the *top* command. The processes are displayed according to the resources used.

An important skill a hacker should possess is the ability to multi-process. Fortunately, Kali distribution allows multiprocessing. The hacker may be working on the scanner and, at the same time, exploiting. The kernel will control the priority of a process. However, the *nice* command is used to manipulate the priority of a process to the kernel. In other words, you can use the *nice* command to recommend that a process should be of a higher rank in priority. The values for *nice* is between -20 to+19, zero being the default value.

Some processes are worth killing. This is because they consume a whole lot of many system resources and display unusual behavior such as freezing. This type of process is often referred to as a zombie process. This is a problematic process that needs to be solved for you to focus on helpful processes. To stop this zombie process, use the *kill* command. There are several ways to kill a process, and each has its kill number. Some of the widely used look signals are SIGHUP 1, SIGINT 2, SIGTERM15, SIGQUIT3, and SIGKILL9.

SIGHUP 1is referred to as the Hang up (HUP) signal, ending the marked-out process and restarting it with the same PID. SIGINT2 is the interrupt signal. It is referred to as a weak kill signal that is not trusted to work. However, it sometimes works. SIGTERM15 is the termination signal, which is the *kill* command kill signal by design. SIGQUIT3 is referred to as the core dump, ending the process and saving the process information in memory. SIGKILL9 is the perfect kill signal. It forces the process to stop by sending it to a particular device.

In Linux, all running commands are executed within a shell. When you start a command, the shell waits until it is accomplished before tendering another command prompt.

You can run a process in the background instead of waiting for it to complete in that terminal. If you go back to the terminal, you will still find that process running in the background.

To move a process running in the background to the foreground, use the foreground or fg command. The fg command will require you to supply the PID of the process you want to transfer to the foreground. For instance, if the PID of the process is 2554, you will include it in your command: Kali> **fg 2554.** You can use the *ps* command to find out the PID of your process.

Hackers may need to schedule processes to execute at a specific time of the day. They may want to set up a script that frequently runs to detect vulnerabilities. Scheduling activities will enable you to run a task without necessarily having to be there. There are three ways this can be achieved in Linux. You can use the *at,* or the *cron* commands.

The *at* command is a background process helpful in scheduling an activity to run at a specific time in the future. The *cron* and *crontab* command is suitable for scheduling activities to happen daily, weekly, or monthly.

The *cron* daemon examines the *cron* table for the commands to run at specific periods. We can modify the *cron* table to set a task that should be executed frequently at a particular time, day, week, or month.

You need to enter the tasks into the *cron* table for you to schedule them. There are seven fields in the *cron* table. To schedule a time, the first five are needed; the sixth field specifies the user, and the seventh field is used for the complete route to the command you want to execute. The five-time field portrays different segments of time. The five-time fields are represented below:

- Minute.   0-59

- Hour   0-23

- Day of the month 1-31

- Month.   1-12

- Day of the week. 0-7

For instance, you can schedule the *cron* table to scan for commerce open ports at 12 am, Friday to Sunday. We need first to understand the format of scheduling. The *cron table* file has done the labeling for you, and this makes the task of scheduling easier.

The first to the fifth field divides time into segments; the sixth specifies the user, also known as the *root,* and the seventh deals with the script.

Chapter Nine

Scripting

A n indispensable skill a professional hacker should possess is scripting. Hackers must be proficient in using commands, especially through multiple tools. To be efficient in scripting, a hacker should have the ability to script in any of the commonly used scripting languages such as Python, Ruby, or Perl. This chapter will deal with both bash scripting and Python scripting. We will be starting with bash scripting.

In bash scripting, a *shell* is a connection between the user and the operating system that helps you to manage files and operate commands, programs, and so on. The benefit of *shell* is that you can operate it directly from the system without an abstraction such as a GUI, which enables you to alter your task to what suits you. There are different types of shells obtainable for Linux. They include the C shell, the Bourne-again shell or bash, the Korn shell, and the Z shell. Of all these shells, the bash shell is obtainable in almost all Linux distribution, hence, our focus on bash scripting. For the purpose of text editing, you will need any of the Linux text editors suitable for you. You can use any of these: *vim, gedit, vi, Kate, emacs, Leafpad,* and the likes.

To start scripting, you need to choose which interpreter you want to use for the script. **To** do this, you will have to enter a *shebang,* represented by a hash mark and an exclamation mark like this: *#!.* To indicate that you want the operating system to work with the bash shell interpreter, type it this way: *#!/bin/bash*. The next step is to type *echo,* a Linux command that signals the system to repeat what follows. The text to echo back will be in double quotation marks. For instance, if we want to echo back *programming,* type: ***echo "programming."*** Then save the file and exit from the text editor. The text file is not yet executable after it is being saved. It is, therefore, necessary to set execute permission. By design, the bash script is not executable, not even to the owner. To set execute permission, type the following: Kali>**chmod 755 programming.**

It is necessary to understand an essential tool in hacking known as Nmap, and this tool is, by design, installed on Kali. Nmap is used for investigating a system to determine if it is connected to the network and explores what ports are accessible. The format to run a Nmap is: nmap <type of scan><Target IP><optionally, target port>.

The most dependable Nmap scan is the TCP connect scan denoted by -sT device in Nmap. If your IP address, for instance, is 175.988.257.2, and assuming port 3306 is open, you can type this:

nmap -sT 175.988.257.2

Furthermore, a hacker must be familiar with the common in-built bash commands such as:

- cd
- break
- bg
- .
- exit
- exec
- eval
- echo
- continue
- readonly
- read
- pwd
- getopts
- jobs
- fg
- export
- test
- shift
- set
- umask

- type

- trap

- times

- [

- wait

- unset

While some of these commands have been explained previously, a breakdown of the command functions is highlighted below:

- cd - it changes directory

- break - it exits the current loop

- bg -it puts a process in the background

- . - this dot executes a shell script

- exit - it ends the shell

- exec - it executes the next command without creating a new process

- eval - it executes the next expression

- echo - it unfurls the command argument

- continue - it resumes the current loop

- readonly - it interprets variable as read-only

- read -it reads a line from standard input

- pwd - it unfurls the current directory

- getopts - splits argument to the shell script

- jobs - it lists background jobs

- fg - it buttons a job to the foreground

- export - it makes a variable available to other programs

- test - it examines arguments

- shift - it moves the parameters to the left

- set - it lists all variables

- unmask - it changes the default authorization for a new file

- type - it displays how arguments would be interpreted as a command

- trap - it traps a signal

- times - it prints the user and systems time

- [- it performs a conditional test

- wait - it waits for a background process to complete

- unset - it deletes values from a variable

Another scripting language commonly used by hackers is Python. Most of the hacking tools, such as sqlmap, the social engineer toolkit, w3af, scapy, and many more, are written in Python.

Python is essential in hacking because it has some features that make it useful for this purpose. It has some in-built components of codes that are home functional and can be reused. Pythons have more than one thousand in-built modules. Its movies make the building of hacking tools very simple.

The advantage of installing python is that it comes with powerful packages such as numeric and math modules, cryptographic services, interaction with internet protocols, file handling, internet data handling, and exception handling. Apart from these packages, there are other modules referred to as the third-party modules and Python allows for them. This is another reason a hacker would like to use Python.

To download and install packages, you will need a package manager known as Pip Installs Packages (pip). To install pip from Kali repository, type: Kali>**apt-get install Python 3- pip.** To download modules from PyPi, enter this: Kali>**pip3 install < package name>**

To be sure where your package is stored on your system, enter the following command: kali>**pip3 show pysnmp.** To install unpacked packages that have not yet been installed, enter this command: kali>**python set up.py install.**

To install a third-party module developed by another Python domain, use *wget* to get it from anywhere it is being stored online. Use the *python set up.py install* command.

Furthermore, Python can be created using the text editor. You can use the leafpad text editor or Integrated development environments (IDE). An IDE functions like the text editor with other functions such as debugging, compiling, and color-coding functions. One of the available IDEs is *Jetbrain's pyCharm.* This is an exceptional IDE with a lot of capabilities that make Python easier to operate. To gain mastery in Python scripting, Jetbrain's pyCharm is very useful for you.

You need to get familiar with some concepts in Python scripting because this will enable you to understand better how this hacking tool works. One of these concepts is *variables.* A variable is one of the fundamental data types in programming. It is connected to a specific value to the extent that when you use it in your program, it invokes the connected value.

If you want to inform your system that it should use the python interpreter to execute your program, type the following: #! /usr/bin/Python 3. You need to change the value to your name and enclose it in quotation marks. However, you have to authorize yourself before you execute this program, and you need the *chmod* command to do that. Type this command: Kali> **chmod 755 programming on going.py.** To execute your script, start the script name with a period and forward slash. To execute it, type this: Kali>**./programming on going. Py.**

Another concept you need to get acquainted with is *comments.* Comments are words, sentences, or paragraphs that analyze what the code is supposed to do. Comments can be useful when you come back to your covered years late, and you do not remember what it should do. It is very useful also for programmers to analyze what a block of codes does or to describe the logic behind pretending a particular method of coding. Comments help us to explain code to ourselves (the user) as well as to other programmers or users.

We need to consider another concept in Python scripting known as *functions.* Functions are bits of Code that execute a specific action. There are about thousands of functions available in Python scripting. Some of them are: float (), exit(), len(), int (), max(), help(), open(), range(), sorted(), type(), and so on.

- float - it returns its argument as a floating-point number

- exit - it leaves a program

- len - it returns the number of components in a list or dictionary

- int - it returns the integer portion of its argument

- max - it returns the maximum value from its argument

- help - it displays help on the object explained by its argument

- open - it opens the file in the mode explained by its argument

- range - it returns a list of integers between two values explained by its argument

- sorted - it takes a list of an argument and takes it back with its components in order.

- type - it returns the type of its argument, for instance, file, function or method.

Also, you will come across *modules* in Python scripting. It has been mentioned above in several instances. A module is simply a division of code stored into a different file in order for you to use it as many times as you will need it without having to type it out again.

To store multiple different objects, a lot of computing languages use *arrays*. An Array is a list of values that can be regained, substituted, or deleted in several ways by referring to a specific value in the array through its position in its index. Python, just like many other programming domains, starts counting its index from zero. Therefore, the first element in the list is index 0; the second is index 1, and so on. The most widely used implementation of an array in Python is known as *list*. The list can provide successive components when you run through it. Lists are very useful because you will be able to look through them and find certain values, print them out or take values from one list and fix them into another list.

Hackers often use a method known as *banner grabbing* to explore vital information about what application is running on a port. A *banner* is what an application presents when someone or something is connected to it. The first thing you need to do is to import the socket modules so that you can use its tools. A socket enables a passage for the system nodes to interact with each other. One is usually a server and the other, a client. You can then create a new variable, *s* representing the *socket* class. In this way, you do not have to reference the full *socket.socket* format anytime we want to use the *socket* class. Then, we use the *connect* method from the socket module to make a network connection to a specific IP and port. After connecting to the IP and port, you can do so many things. You can use the receive method(*recv)* to read bytes of data from the socket and save them in a variable known as *answer.* You can then print the contents of that variable to the screen with the *print()* function to view what data has been passed through that socket. You can use SSH to read the banner into your *answer* variable. To create a simple banner grabbing python script, enter this command: Kali>**./ProgrammingSSHBannerGrab.py,** assuming the script to be displayed is *programming.*

In Python scripting, dictionaries function like associative arrays in other programming languages. Dictionaries store a number of items and supply each item a label to use and revert to them individually.

A dictionary can be used to store a user ID or to check for vulnerabilities related to a particular host. We can use a control structure, such as a *for loop,* to run through the entire dictionary. Each dictionary component is designated to a variable until the end is reached.

Control Statements

These are statements that are used to make decisions based on some conditions. Some of the control statements that would be examined in this chapter include the **if** statement and the **if....else** statement.

Like every other programming language, the **if statement** is a conditional statement used to check if a statement is true or false. The if condition statement is written in this format:

> **if   conditional expression**
>
> **run this code if the expression is true**

Having input these statements, if the condition is true, the if condition evaluates it to be true. After this evaluation, run the **control back** command. However, if the statement is not true, there won't be any need to execute the control back. Hence, it is skipped.

Another conditional statement that can be used to determine the truth or falsity of a statement is the **if....else**. The format of this command is similar to this:

> **if conditional expression**

*** # run this code when the condition is met

else

*** # run this code when the condition is not met

Like the if conditional statement, in the **if....else**, if the statement is true, the result is executed in the **control back.** However, if it is false, the result is executed in the **control back** that comes after the else statement.

Loop

Another structure to take note of in Python is the Loop. The loop allows the operator or programmer to repeat a code multiple times. The two loops that are widely used in Python include the **while** loop and the **for** loop.

The **while** loop examines a Boolean expression. A Boolean expression is an expression that can be evaluated to be either true or false. The **while** loop continues the evaluation and execution process, while the statement is executed to be true. If the statement is true, the control block continues to run.

The **for** loop is used to assign a value from a dictionary, list, string or other iterable structures to an index variable. For instance, a **for** loop can be used to attempt a password until it gets a match.

Exceptions and Password Crackers

Exceptions are like code errors. They disrupt the flow of the code either because it is wrong, or it was not inputted in the right manner. To deal with an error or exception, we would be using the **exception handling**. This handling is a code that presents an error problem and handles error-related cases. The exception handling tool in python includes **try/except** blocks.

The **try/except** block functions as the name implies. The **try** aspect of the block tries a code, and if the code is wrong, the **except** block corrects the errors. This is similar to the way the **if...else** block functions. For example, the **try/except** block can be used in a password cracker to try a password. If the password does not match, the except block will move this process to the next password without causing any error.

Chapter Ten

Software Manipulation

In Linux or any operating system, software manipulation is one of the ground laying tasks. It is not all software that comes with your distribution. Therefore, there will be a need for you to install them. You may also need to delete some software that is not useful for you so that you can have sufficient space in your hard drive.

Some software depends on other software to function, and you can easily download anything you want simultaneously in a software package. Installing a software package implies that all the files within it have also been installed.

There are three crucial methods for adding new software. They are GUI based installation managers, apt package manager, and git. It is important for you, as a hacker or a prospective hacker, to understand how these methods operate, hence, the need to discuss them extensively.

GUI-Based Installation

The latest version of Kali no longer comes with the GUI-based software applications; however, you can install them with the *apt-get* command. The two commonest GUI-based installation devices are Gdebi and Synaptic. To install snort, you need first to install

Synaptic. Type: Kali>**apt-get install Synaptic.** After you have successfully installed Synaptic, you can open the settings (Synaptic Package Manager). This will open a window. Type *snort* into the search window and click **search.** Then scroll down and get the package you are searching for. Click the **Apply** tab in the box close to snort. Finally, Synaptic will install *snort* from the repository together with necessary packages.

Repositories are the servers that hold the software for specific distributions of Linux. Almost all distributions have their own repositories of software, and the Kali repository has a huge amount of hacking software.

Apt for Software

In Linux distributions, including Kali, Advanced Packaging Tool (APT) is by design a software manager. Its basic command is apt-get, and it can be used to install new software packages. Also, you can use it to upgrade and update software. **To** know if the package you need is available before downloading it, check it from your repository or archive. To search whether the package is available, type: apt-cache search keyword. If you want to remove software, use apt-get with the *remove* option, and then add the name of the software you want to remove. For instance, if you want to remove Synaptic, type: Kali>**apt-get remove Synaptic.** You will be asked whether you want to continue with the removing process: Do you want to continue [y/n]? Type *y* to uninstall, however, if you want to keep the Synaptic just in case you will need it again, you can reinstall it since the *remove* command does not automatically remove the configuration files. But if you want to remove both the configuration files and the package, use the *purge* option. Type this: Kali>**apt-get purge Synaptic.** You will be asked whether you want to continue, just like in the case of removing software, type *y* to indicate that you want to continue. The software repository or archive will be updated intermittently due to the new versions of existing software. However, the updates do not get to you automatically.

Furthermore, you can update your personal system by typing the apt-get command and the word *update*. This command will run through the packages on your system and investigate whether updates are available.

To achieve this, type: Kali>**apt-get update.**

To upgrade the current packages on your system, type: Kali> **apt-get upgrade.**

Every package on your system recognized by apt will be upgraded. Upgrading takes quite a long while. Therefore, you might not be able to use your system for a long period. In the output, you will see that your system appraises the amount of hard drive space required for the software package. You will be asked whether you want to continue upgrading, type *y* to indicate that you want to continue.

Using Git to Install Software

Some software that cannot be found in any of the repositories can be found on git. It provides a website where developers can share their software with others to download and provide feedback; visit this website: https://www.github.com to download any software shared by developers with others. For instance, if you want to download *Metasploit* through git, enter this command: Kali>**git clone https://www.github.com/ballet/metasploit.git.** Use the command *ls-l* to be certain that it has been downloaded.

Chapter Eleven

File Compression And
Storage Device Management

For easier sending and downloading of large scripts and files, a hacker needs to learn how to compress and combine multiple files into a single file. This process is synonymous with the zip format from the Windows domain. The zip format compresses files to make them smaller for transmitting through the internet or the media. Compression makes data smaller, hence, demanding less storage capacity and making data faster and easier to transmit. There are two major categories of compression: lossy and lossless.

Lossy compression is highly operative in decreasing the size of files. However, the wholeness of the information or data is lost. This form of compression can best be appreciated for graphics, audio, and video files because a little difference is barely noticeable. Examples of lossy compression algorithms are png, jpg, mp3, and mp4. When data wholeness is of high importance, lossy compression is substandard.

It is much more important to a hacker than a compression ratio; therefore, our focus will be on lossless compression.

Before compressing files, it is important that you first merge them into an archive. The *tar* (tape archive) command is used more frequently when archiving files. This command functions like the nonmodern days of computing when tapes are used to store data. It creates a single file from multiple files, which is known as a tarfile or a tarball.

For better comprehension, let us assume you have four script files which are: *programming 1, programming 2, programming 3,* and *programming 4.* You will see some information concerning the files from the directory that binds them, including the size of the files. Assuming you want to send these files to another hacker working with you to execute a project, create a single archive file through this command:

Kali> *tar -cvf programming.tar programming 1 programming 2 programming 3 programming 4*

To illustrate this, the *tar* is the archiving command being used with four options. The c option indicates *create, v represents verbose.* This lists the files that *tar* is operating with. *f means* write to the following file. Then give the new archive the file name you want it to have. Through this command, the four files are merged into a single file.

Linux has various commands that can be used to compress files. Commands such as bzip2, gzip, and compress are very effective in achieving this purpose. Each of these commands uses different algorithms and have different compression ratios. *Compress* is the fastest of these three, while gzip is the slowest.

Gzip is the most widely used compression utility in Linux. To compress your file, you need to ensure that you are in the directory that stores the file. If, for instance, you want to compress your *programming* file, use this command: Kali> **gzip programming*.** The wide card * is used to indicate that Linux should apply the command to all the files that start with *programming.* When a long listing is done on the directory, the file size has been compressed. We can then decompress the file using the *GNU unzip* command (gunzip). To decompress the file, use this command: kali>**gunzip programming*.**

The next widely used compression tool in Linux is bzip2. This tool is related to gzip. However, it has better compression ratios, and the compressed file will be smaller. To compress your *programming* file, you can compress your file by entering this command: Kali>**bzip2 programming.***

Enter the following to uncompress the compressed file: Kali>**bunzip2 programming.*** Then the file returns to its usual size.

Another compression command is *compress.* It is likely the least widely used compression utility. To use it, enter the following: Kali> **compress programming.*** To decompress this file, enter Kali>**uncompress programming.***

An outstanding Linux archiving command that is so beneficial in the world of technology is the *dd* command. This command provides a bit by bit copy of the data or file system. This command is so useful that it has access even to deleted files. It makes the recovery of files possible.

This command is essential for forensic hacking to provide a physical copy of the hard drive with deleted files and other tools that can help investigate or find evidence against the hacker.

The principal format for the *dd* command is *dd if=inputfile of=outputfile.*

Linux operates with logical labels. These labels defer based on when they are mounted. In other words, different labels can be given to the same hard drive at different times and at different locations, based on where and when it is mounted. Drives are occasionally divided into sections referred to as *partitions,* which are usually denoted by labeling structures with numbers. When there is more than one hard drive in systems, Linux names them by amplifying the last letter in alphabetical order. The first drive is *sda;* the second drive is *sdb,* the third drive is sdc, and so on.

It is important to note that Linux represented floppy drives as **fdo** and hard drives as **hda**. Also, Newer Serial ATA (SATA) interface drives and Small Computer System Interface (SCSI) hard drives are represented as sda.

To control information, some files can be divided into partitions. You may need to share resources or relieve the designed authorization. These actions may cause you to separate your hard drive. Linux numbers each partition with a minor number that comes after the drive designation. Following this, the first partition on the first SATA drive would be sda1; the second would be sda2, the third would be sda3, and so on.

You may sometimes want to view the partition on your Linux system to see which ones you have and what capacity is available in each. You can achieve this using the -l switch with *fdisk*: Kali:>**fdisk- l**

The result that pops on the screen, for instance, may be that you have sda1, sda2,sda3, and sda5 listed in the first few lines. These devices are in your virtual disk, which could have a 20GB capacity.

One thing to note about the naming of device files on the /dev directory is that the first position contains either c or *b*. These alphabets represent the ways that devices transmit data in and out. The *c* represents character or character devices. Character devices are external devices that communicate with the system by sending and receiving data characters. *b* represents block devices. They interact in a box of data and entail devices like DVD drives and hard drives. These devices need high-speed data. They send and receive data in blocks, using many bytes at a time.

Furthermore, there are some concepts in Linux known as *mounting* and *unmounting*. The term *mount* originated from the early days of computing when storage tapes had to be physically mounted to the computer system. Some modern operating systems such as Linux usually have a hard drive or flash drive attached to the file system. A storage device has to be first connected to the file system physically and then logically attached to the file system so that the data will be made available to the operating system. This implies that the storage device, when connected physically, does not cover up for the logical connection if it is not logically connected and vice versa. You must learn the skill of mounting a storage device. To mount a drive on the storage device, use the *mount* command. Note that the mount point for the device should be an empty directory. The reason is that the mounted device will block the contents of the directory, making them invisible. To mount the new hard drive sdb2, using the media directory, for instance, enter Kali>**mount/dev/ sdb2 /media**

Almost everyone who has used the Windows operating system will be familiar with *unmounting*. Before removing a flash drive from your system, you eject it so as not to cause damage to the files on your system. Eject performs the same function as unmounting.

You can unmount a second hard drive by entering the umount command. Enter: Kali>**umount/dev/sdb2**.

It is noteworthy that unmounting a busy device can lead to error. Therefore, when a device is reading or writing, do not unmount.

How to Monitor Filesystem

Monitoring filesystem is a skill that every hacker must endeavor to have. This is because storage devices are prone to errors. So, with this skill, the system administrator would be able to get some vital information about the mounted disk and check for errors. The errors can be easily fixed before it causes havoc to the system.

To get information on the mounted disk, the **df** (disk free) command would be used. This command allows you to access the information stored on the mounted device or hard disk. To check a different disk, type the **df** command and follow this up with drive representation.

To check for errors, use the **fsck** command. However, before running this command, you would need to specify the filesystem type and the device type. This can be done by running the **ext2** command. Ensure that the drive is unmounted before running the filesystem command. Failure to do this can lead to error.

Chapter Twelve

Directory Authorization

L INUX has processes for directory access and for securing data or information. The security structure grants the system user or the file owner to protect their file or personal information from unauthorized access by allowing select users' authorizations to read, write, and execute files. This chapter focuses on how to control and change authorization on files and directors for select users, how to set unique authorizations, and how to set default file or information and directory authorizations.

There are different types of users in Linux. We have the root user and other users who are grouped according to their shared similar domain. The root user has unlimited power and can do anything on the system. The other types of users do not have limited power or authorization and might never have the access that the root user has. These groups might be IT, finance, engineering, businesses, and so on. The reason behind this is to put people with similar interests into the same group for them to gain relevant authorization. This, in turn, is for security purposes. By design, the root user is part of the root group.

There must be a specific level of authorization for every file and directory distributed to the different individuals using it. The three levels of authorization are:

- **Authorization to read:** this allows for authorization to just open and view a file.

- **Authorization to write:** this grants the user's opportunity to view and edit a file.

- **Authorization to execute:** this enables users to run a file, although the file may not be viewed or edited.

Furthermore, a root user can grant other users some level of authorization based on what they need the files for. When a file is generated, it is the user, who generated it, which is the owner of the file. However, you can transfer the ownership of the file to another user so that they can have the ability to control authorization. To change the owner, use the *chown (*change owner) command. Type:

Kali>chown(1) Charles(2)/ tmp/Charlesfile.

This command contains the name of the users we want to transfer ownership to, the location, and then the name of the file.

You can also transfer ownership of the group; however, various hackers can work together to achieve maximum results on a project. Using groups in this scenario is inevitable.

The root group needs the hacking devices while the security group needs the defensive devices like an intrusion detection system. The root group will need to transfer the ownership to the security group so that the security group can have access to the program or file. Assuming the name of the program or file is *storage* device, to change ownership, type:

Kali>chgrp(1) security (2) storage device.

To check if the distributions have worked, check the file's authorizations. Also, if you want to determine what authorizations to what users for a directory or file, use the *ls* command with the - *l (long)* device to display the contents of a directory on a long layout, which will contain the authorizations. To check for authorizations, use this format: Kali>*ls- l /file/.* The output of this includes the following:

- The owner of the file

- The name of the file

- The size of the file in bytes

- The file type

- The number of links

- The authorizations on the file for owner

- Users and groups

- When the file was generated or last altered.

Apart from the three levels of authorizations mentioned above, Linux has another three unique levels of authorizations that are more intricate. These unique authorizations are: sticky bit, set user ID(SUID), and set group ID.

The sticky bit is an authorization bit that you can create on a directory to enable a user to rename or delete files within that directory. Although sticky bit is ignored by some modern operating systems like Linux, you should get acquainted with it because you can come in contact with it in the Linux domain. It is a descendant of older Unix systems. It is referred to as being obsolete.

We have established that a user can only run a file only if they are authorized to run it. It is also possible for the users to read and write authorizations but will not be able to execute it. However, this does not happen in all cases. The set user ID permits any user to execute the file with the authorization of the owner. However, the authorizations do not stretch beyond the operation of that file. To create the set user ID, type 4 before the normal authorizations. A file with the code 398 will be represented as 4398 with the setting of set user ID. Use this command to create a set user ID: chmod 4398 *filename.*

Set group ID also allows authorization, not of the file's owner, but the file owner's group. In other words, through a set group ID, a user without execute authorization can execute a file if the owner is a member of the group that has the authorization to execute it.

Every member of the group can execute the files because the directory is shared by several users. The service group ID is created by typing 2 before the normal authorizations. Therefore, a file with code 398 will be represented as 2398 to set the group ID. Create a set group ID with this command: chmod 2398 *filename.*

Hackers, special permissions, and privileges.

As a hacker, you can explore other special permissions through the Linux privilege escalation. The privilege escalation allows a user to gain access to root privileges and all related permissions. Once you gain access to these privileges, you can run any activities on the system. One of the ways to gain this privilege is through the SUID bit. This bit can be set by the system administrator or user. The purpose of setting the bit is to gain access to the root privilege. For example, most scripts that require password reset have SUID bit. As a hacker, you can use the bit to gain temporary root privileges. With this, you have the power to carry out malicious activities like gaining access to the passwords at **/etc/shadow.**

To see how this works, we would be using the **find** command to search for some files with the SUID set. Here is how the command would be run:

kali >find / -user root -perm -4000

The output of this search would reveal numerous files with SUID bit. Next, we will navigate to where most of these files are kept in the **/usr/bin** directory and run a long search on the directory. After this, we will scroll down to the **sudo** file. In our result, we'll notice that in the first set of permissions, **s** is used in place of the **x.** This is an indication that the SUID bit is set. With this discovery, you have access to the privileges of the root user.

The SUID bit can act as a major security concern to hackers and system administrators. This is because should an attacker gain access to this file, he or she can easily get the password to the Linux system and become privy to vital information. However, it is important to note that Linux has well-developed security that prevents unauthorized access to the system.

How to Check Permissions

The commonest tool used to find out the type of permission granted to a user for a directory or file is the ls command. This command is used alongside the -l tool to display a long list of the contents of a directory or file. The information contained in the displayed content includes:

- The type of file

- The permissions on the file for owners, users, and groups

- The number of links on the file

- The file size in bytes

- The owner of the file

- The name of the file

- The time the file was created or modified.

On the left edges of the displayed content, some seemingly incomprehensible dashes, letters, and strings would be seen. These signs reveal to us whether the item is a directory or a file. It also reveals the type of permission on the file. Most times, directories are represented with a letter **d**, while file is represented with **(-).** These two file types are the most common ones that exist.

The next section of the left edges reveals the permissions. There are three types of permissions in Linux. The first set of permission is for the owner, the second is for the group, and the type is for the users. The three actions that can be performed by each of the permissions include **r** (read), **w** (write), and **x** (execute). The **r** implies that the user or group of users can read the file or directory, the **w** sign means that they can write or modify the directory or file. The third sign **x** means they can execute the file or directory. If these three permissions are represented with a dash, it means that permission has not been given. It is important to note that users can only have permission to execute scripts or binaries.

These three permissions are not unchangeable. As a root user, you can alter any of these three permissions.

How to Change Permissions

The three permissions explained above can be changed using the **chmod** command. However, it is important to note that only the root user or file owner can change permission.

Aside from the **chmod** command, there is a shortcut to changing permission. The shortcut includes using a single number to represent the three permissions. Permissions, like all the processes underlying the operating system, are represented in binaries. As such, the switches for ON and OFF are represented by 1 and 0, respectively. Since the permissions we have are three, the ON and OFF would be represented in three formats. Thus, when all permissions are granted, our binary would be 111.

This type of binary set can be converted into a digit using the octal. Octal is an eight-digit system of numbers beginning with 0 and ending with 7. One octal is equal to a set of three binary digits. Therefore our binary set for **rwx** can be represented with one digit. All the three permissions would give us the octal 777.

Now by passing the chmod command with three octal digits, each representing a permission, and then follow this with the file name, we can change the permission for each user.

How to Change Permission With UGO

While most users prefer to use the numeric number for changing permissions, others favor the use of **chmod's** symbolic method. It is this method that is referred to as the UGO meaning users, groups, and others. **Chmod's** symbolic method is often favored because it is believed to be more intuitive. Nevertheless, both the numeric method and the UGO work well.

Using the UGO is quite simple. All you have to do is input the chmod command and follow this with any permission you want to change. This implies that you will choose either **u** for users, **g** for group, or **o** for others. Next, you will add any of the following:

- Add a permission

- Remove a permission

- Set a permission

Next, include any of the permission you want to change and the name of the file you want to change it to. This command would be in this format:

kali >chmod u-w hacker.expert

The above command says remove (-) the write (w) permission from hacker.expert for the user (u).

This command can also be used to change multiple permissions. The format would be as follows:

chmod u+x, o+x hacker.expert

This command tells Linux to execute permissions for both users and others.

Another important thing to take note of is how to execute permission on a new tool. As a hacker, you would often need to download new hacking tools. Whenever you do, Linux would automatically set the default permissions of all directories and files as 777 and 666, respectively. Hence, whenever you download a file, you would not be able to execute it immediately. If you try to, the response will be "permission denied."

Therefore to execute permission on a new device, you will need to use the **chmod** command. For instance, assuming you download a new hacking tool with the name newhackingtool. To execute permission on this tool, you will run the following command:

kali >chmod 766 newhackertool

Changing Default Permission with Mask

In the explanation above, it would be noticed that Linux automatically assigns base permission, usually 777 for directories and 666 for files. These two default base permissions can be changed with **umask** method. This method stands for the permission you want to remove. The umask is a three digits decimal number. Each of the numbers represents the three permissions. To get the number that would represent each permission, the **umask** number would be subtracted from the default permission number. What this implies is that when a new directory or file is created, the permission of that directory or file is set to default value minus the value in **umask**.

In Linux, umask is usually preconfigured as 022. When this digit is subtracted from the 666 for file or 777 for the directory, we would have 644 for file and 755 for the directory. However, this value is not universal. A user can decide to change the value to any digit of his or her choice. To do this, edit the file **/home/username/.profile** and set the **umask** digit to any one of your choices. When this is done, only the user's group would have permission to the file or directory.

Chapter Thirteen

Anonymity and Tracking Security

In present-day technology, tracking has become a common occurrence in networking. Areas such as Google, websites, emails, and online searches are frequently being tracked. A hacker needs to be knowledgeable in how to restrict tracking as well as staying anonymous on the internet to curb this prevalent monitoring.

A hacker should be able to stay anonymous when navigating the World Wide Web. There are basically four methods a user can employ in achieving anonymity, namely: Virtual private networks, the onion network, private encrypted email, and proxy servers. These methods may not totally provide a perfect security measure; however, they can make out difficult for trackers to gain access to the files.

There are several ways your activities on the internet can be tracked. We must identify the commonest and effortless way they can be tracked to help us guard against being a victim. One of the ways your activities can be easily tracked is through your IP address. Files transferred from your system are usually tagged with your IP address. When sending files through the internet, the IP addresses of both the file source and destination are captured. As the file journeys through the internet, any internet user who comes in contact with the file can see where it is coming from, where it is at the moment, and where it is going. To keep track of how your file journeys from you to its destination, use the *traceroute* command. Type *traceroute* and the destination of the IP address: Kali> ***traceroute google.com.*** The command will send out files to the destination and track the path of those files. We will now discuss these four methods of staying anonymous mentioned above.

Virtual Private Networks

One of the operative ways your web traffic can stay anonymous and safe is by using a Virtual Private Network (VPN). The purpose of a VPN is to connect to a middle network device like a router that transmits your traffic to its final destination tagged with the IP address of the router. Some of the most popular VPN services are IPVanish, Express VPN, CyberGhost, Private Internet Access, TorGuard, Golden Frog VPN, Nord VPN, Pure VPN, Hide My Ass VPN, and Buffered VPN.

An advantage of a VPN is that all your traffic is coded when it leaves your system, thereby guiding you against snooping or investigation. It is best to use a VPN that promises not to log files or information so that the VPN owner does not disclose your identity when pressured to do so.

The Onion Network

The US Office of Naval Research (ONR), in the 1990s, planned to design a method for anonymity regarding navigating the internet for spying purposes. They intended to invent a network of routers different from the internet routers so that they could code the traffic. The essence of it is that anyone viewing the traffic would not be able to determine the source or destination of the file. In 2002, this research became known as *'The Onion Router(Tor) project.* Today, it is now available to users for security and anonymity while navigating the web. The Onion Router project or Tor codes the file, the destination, and the transmitter's IP address of each file. The information is coded at each hop and decoded when it gets to the receiver. If another user intercepts the traffic, they can only see the IP address of the former hop; also, the website owner can only view the IP address of the lady router that transmitted the traffic. This enables security and anonymity throughout the internet. To install the Tor browser, visit: https

Private Encrypted Email

To secure your personal information on free commercial services like Gmail, Yahoo, Google, and other services that require your email, use the encrypted email. *ProtonMail* encrypts your email from browser to browser. It is designed in a way that even the Proton Mail supervisors cannot access your email. You need to encrypt your email because the servers of the email provider, such as Google, can still have access to your email even with https.

Proxy Servers

Another trick to obtaining anonymity on the internet is to use proxies, which act as the middlemen for traffic. The user connects to a proxy, and the traffic is given the address of the proxy before it transmits. When the traffic returns from the destination, the proxy transmits the traffic back to the source. This implies that traffic seems to come from the proxy and not from the originating IP address.

Although the proxy will log your traffic, a snooper would have to be rigorous in their search for authorization to access the logs. Kali Linux uses a proxy tool referred to as proxychains. To set up the proxychains, use the following command:

kali >proxychains <the command you want proxied> <arguments>

How to set the proxies in a config file

In Linux, the proxychains are managed by the config file. The specific config file that manages the proxies is the **/etc/proxychains.conf**. To access the proxychain, you would have to open the config file; this can be done by typing the following command:

kali >leafpad /etc/proxychains.conf

This command sets up the proxy and gets it ready to be used. However, with this command, what is used is only a single command. To add more proxies, go to http://www.hidemy.name, to get some proxy IPs. When you do, add the proxies using the following command:

> [ProxyList]
>
> # add proxy here...
>
> socks4 114.134.186.12 22020
>
> socks4 188.187.190.59 8888
>
> socks4 181.113.121.158 335551

After this, save your configuration and run this command: kali >proxychains firefox www.hackers-arise.com. The difference between these multiple configurations and the single one would not be obvious. However, your package is currently traveling through several proxies.

Dynamic Chaining

This is a method used to keep the multiple proxies on a system working effectively. Dynamic proxy is a configuration that runs the traffic through all the proxies on the list. During this process, when one of the proxies is not responding, dynamic chaining enables the configuration to run to the next working proxy without creating or recording any errors. Without the dynamic chaining, a failing proxy can crash the entire configuration. To set the **dynamic_chain**, search for the **dynamic_chain line**. Usually, this line is line 10. When you locate the line, uncomment it. Also, ensure that you uncomment the **strict_chains**. This process enables the dynamic chaining of multiple proxies. With the dynamic chaining, you will enjoy a trouble-free hacking.

Random Chaining

This process allows the multiple proxy configurations to randomly select some IP addresses and use them to create the proxychain. Like the dynamic chaining, random chaining also allows the traffic to skip a non-functioning proxy to the next functioning one. To create the random chaining, go to the **/etc/proxychains.conf** and uncomment both the **dynamic_chain** and the **strict_chain**. However, ensure you add the sign # to the beginning of each line. Next, go to the random_chain and uncomment it. After this, go to the **chain_len** and uncomment it, next write the number of proxies you want in your random chain. With this process, you have created a random chain of proxies. Also, like dynamic chaining, this process enhances your anonymity.

Note: when choosing your proxies, ensure you choose meticulously. If your purpose of using the proxy is to remain anonymous, it is not advisable to use free proxies. This is because the free proxy can reveal your details. Also, unethical hackers often used paid-for proxies to carry out their act.

Although the IP address of some of the free proxies is usually anonymous, the producer of the proxy can easily access your details. In a situation whereby cases of hacking arise, the producer can give your details out to the law enforcement agents. These are some of the reasons it is not advisable to use free proxies.

Chapter Fourteen

Use And Misuse Service

L inux system has several services preinstalled. By services, we mean those applications that execute in the background, and you can access to operate on at any time. The most widely used of all these services is the Apache Web Server, which is highly useful for controlling, creating, and opening web servers.

You can start or stop some services through the GUI in Kali Linux, but some services require the use of command, like we have treated some of them in the preceding chapters. It is also applicable in this chapter as we examine how services can be used or misused.

To control services, type: service *servicename* start/stop/restart. Type: Kali>**service apache2 start,** to start Apache Web Server. Type: Kali>**service apache2 stop,** to stop it, and type: Kali> **service apache 2 restart,** to restart it.

These are basically for services that are crucial to hackers; they are Apache Web Server, MySQL, OpenSSH, and PostgreSQL. We will examine these services one after the other to understand how they operate.

Apache Web Server

Apache Web Server is a widely used service in Linux systems. Any Linux operating should be familiar with it because it is found in more than 60 percent of web servers across the world. A hacker should be familiar with the fundamentals of Apache, starting from knowing its usefulness in setting up a web server that could serve as malware to other users who visit your site, or you could substitute traffic to your site through the misuse of the Domain Name System.

By default, Apache is installed in Kali Linux. However, if you do not have it installed in your Linux distribution, you will need first to install it. To achieve this, type: Kali> **apt-get install apache2.** To start Apache, using Kali, go to *applications,* then to *Services,* and then to *HTTPD*. To get the same result, you can add well type this command: Kali> **service apache2 start.** After starting it, enter *http://localhost/* in your browser to bring up the web page. After the web page is brought up, you can now alter it to suit your specification. Then, you may want to edit the *index.html File* and fill in any information you want. Create a page and save the file with any name you desire. Your text editor will prompt you that the file now exists. To open the file again, enter *http://localhost/*, and you will see your web page just exactly as you have created it.

MySQL

The commonest database used for database-driven web applications is MySQL. In modern-day technology, almost all websites are database driven. This implies that MySQL is indispensable for most of the web.

Databases contain essential information and even some confidential information such as the credit card numbers of the users. Since hackers need information and, most especially, confidential information, they are likely to target databases. MySQL is widely open to the public, just like Linux. It is, by default, installed on almost all Linux distributions.

Since it is open, free, and easily accessible, MySQL has become the most preferred database for many web applications such as Wikipedia, Facebook, Twitter, LinkedIn, WordPress, YouTube, and Walmart.com. From these few descriptions of MySQL, a prospective hacker should get inspired to learn more about it.

MySQL is, by default, installed in Kali Linux. However, you can install it if you do not have it in your distribution. To download it, visit *https://www.mysql.com.downloads/.* After this, start your MySQL service by typing the following command: Kali> *service mysql start.* The next thing is to verify yourself by logging in. Enter the following: Kali>*mysql -u root -p.* In the default structure of MySQL, the root user's password is empty. Therefore, this constitutes a great security vulnerability. To rectify this, create a password after your first login. There are various tools in MySQL; these are few of them below:

- *Insert:* for adding a new file

- *Update:* for modifying existing files

- *Select:* for retrieving files

- *Union:* for combining the results of two or more chosen operations

To assign a password, you will first choose a database to work with. To view all the databases available, use this command: mysql>*show databases.* Three different databases come with MySQL. *Information Schema* and *Performance Schema* are administrative databases, while *mysql* is the non- administrative database. For the purpose of this study, we will need the non-administrative database. To start using the MySQL database, type: mysql>*use mysql.* This command links us with MySQL. We can now create a password. To create it, use this format: mysql>*update user set password.*

Furthermore, we can connect to the database we desire by entering: mysql>*use programming,* where *programming* is assumed to be the database name.

How to Access a Remote Database

The following command can be used to gain access to the MySQL database on the localhost: **kali >mysql -u <username> -p**. But before this command can function, the IP address or hostname of the system hosting the MySQL must be provided. An example of a hostname is **kali >mysql -u root -p 192.168.1.101.** The hostname connects us directly to the MySQL instance and asks for the system's password. However, the password phase can be bypassed if you are using a root operating system.

After you have input the password, the MySQL command-line interface(CLI) would be opened. This provides the MySQL prompt needed to access the database. Aside from the MySQL CLI, MySQL also has the GUI interfaces—both native (MySQL Workbench) and third party (Navicat and TOAD for MySQL). As a hacker, the command line provides the best opportunity to access the database.

Now that you have been able to access the database, the next action is to get familiar with the database. To find the database on access, use the following command:

```
mysql >show databases;

+-------------------------------------+

| Database          |

+-------------------------------------+

| information  schema        |

| mysql            |

| credit card numbers         |

| performance_schema       |
```

```
+---------------------------------------+
```

4 rows in set (0.26 sec)

OpenSSH

When building a web server, SSH helps you to connect safely to a terminal on a wireless system, which was a substitute for the unsafe telnet that was rampant years back. SSH means *Secure Shell*. It helps us to generates an access list of users operating with this service, verify users with passwords, and encode all communication. This decreases the operation of unauthorized users. The commonest Linux SSH service is OpenSSH, which is, by default, installed in Kali distribution. To start OpenSSH on your Kali system, enter: Kali>*service ssh start.*

We can use SSH to manage a Raspberry Pi. A Raspberry Pi is a very small credit card system that works exceptionally as a remote spying tool. Ensure that your Raspberry Pi runs the Raspbian operating system. This is just a Linux distribution, particularly designed for the Raspberry Pi CPU. To download Raspbian, visit https. If you have downloaded your Raspbian operating system, connect your Raspberry Pi to a mouse, monitor, and keyboard and connect it to the internet.

As soon as SSH is set, you can begin it on your Raspberry Spy Pi by typing this command: Kali> *service ssh start.*

The next thing is to connect your camera module. As the SSH runs, put the Raspberry Spy somewhere around your home or any location you want to spy on. Ensure it is connected to any local area network through Ethernet cable or via Wi-Fi. To connect to the remote Raspberry Spy Pi through the SSH on your Kali distribution, enter Kali> *ssh pi@989.124.2.787,* where the IP address of your Pi is assumed to be *989.124.2.787.*

Another thing you need to do is to configure the camera. To do so, type the following command: pi> *sudo raspi-config.* A list will pop up on the screen, scroll down and click on *Enable Camera* and press ENTER. Scroll to the bottom of the list and press FINISH and then press ENTER. The configuration device will ask you if you want to reboot, click on *Yes* and press ENTER again. Now, the Raspberry Spy Pi Camera should be set for spying.

PostgreSQL

PostgreSQL is another database service that is free and accessible to the public. It is mostly used in large internet applications because of its ability to manage house workloads. This service was first released in 1996 and supported by a vast group of developers refers to as the PostgreSQL Global Development Group. This service is also, by default, installed in Kali, but if you are using a different distribution, you can use this command: Kali>**apt-get postgres install.**

PostgreSQL is highly essential to a hacker because it is, by design, the most commonly used penetration and hacking device, Metasploit. PostgreSQL is useful for Metasploit because it stores modules and the outcome of scans and exploits for penetration research. To start PostgreSQL, type this command: Kali>**service e postgresql start.** One it starts running, start Metasploit, using this command: Kali> **msfconsole.** When Metasploit starts running, you will see an msf cue.

The next step to take is to connect your Metasploit console to your PostgreSQL by providing some information such as the user, the host, the password, and the database name.

Chapter Fifteen

Kernel Module Operation

One of the major components of all operating systems is the kernel. It is the central nervous system of all operating systems. It manages everything the operating system does, which includes managing the memory, controlling what the users watch on screen as well as controlling the CPU.

By default, the kernel is a guarded area that can be accessed by selected accounts. When users gain access to the kernel, they can alter how the operating system works. It also enables them to destroy the operating system. However, the kernel is a potent tool crucial for functional and security purposes.

In Linux distribution, modules can be altered. It could either be added or removed from the Kernel. Frequently, the kernel will need to be updated, and this could involve installing new devices such as USB devices or Bluetooth devices, and system extensions. In some distributions, you have to compile and reboot the whole kernel before you can add a driver. Still, in Linux distribution, you do not need to compile or reboot because it has the ability to add some modules to the Kernel. These modules are known as loadable kernel modules (LKMs).

Loadable kernel modules can penetrate the smallest level of the Kernel. Having an in-depth knowledge of LKMs is the secret of being an effective hacker. There is a specific form of malware known as a *rootkit,* which is encapsulated in the kernel of the operating system, most times through LKMs. In this way, the hacker can successfully lure a Linux admin into downloading a video or other device driver that had a rootkit in it.

You must understand what kernel operates in your system. To check for this, enter: Kali>**uname- a.** The kernel, for instance, may inform you that your operating system is running a Linux Kali. Others may get different results depending on what type of distribution their systems run. Another way to get this information is to use the *cat* command: Kali>**cat/proc/version**.

There are two major ways to manage kernel modules. The first one is to use a group of commands known as *insert module* or *insmod.* It is designed to operate with modules. The second method is by using the *modprobe* command. To use the *insmod* command, type: Kali>***insmod.*** The outcome of this command is that it lists all the kernel modules and some vital information about their size and what other middle can operate with them. Also, we can either insert or remove modules through *insmod* suite. However, *insmod* suite may not take responsibility for module reliability; therefore, operating with it may cause some instability in your kernel. Due to the shortcoming of this method, modern distributions of Linux have now included the second method known as *modprobe,* which is more reliable and less risky when adding or removing kernel modules. To use the *modprobe* command, type **modeinfo** filled by the module you want to investigate. For instance: Kali>**modeinfo usb.**

Tuning your kernel can help you to protect your kernel against attacks, and can also help you to modify memory allocations. To carry this out, Linux uses the *sysctl* command. Until you reboot the system, all the changes you make with this command is in effect. **To** make the changes remain, you need to edit the configuration file by entering this:/etc/sysctl.conf. However, you need to be very careful in making sure that there are no mistakes before making permanent changes.

How to Find More Information With modinfo

To have an in-depth knowledge of any of the kernel modules, use the **modinfo** command. The command is implemented by including the name of the module you want to know about to the command. For instance, to learn more about the Bluetooth module, the command would be written in this format:

kali >modinfo Bluetooth

The above command would display all the necessary information needed to be able to use the Bluetooth tool. Among the information is the module's dependencies. These include **rfkill** and **crc16**. Dependencies are modules needed for the effectiveness of any tool. They must be installed for the tool to function well. Dependencies also help to know the module and kernel versions the module is developed for. This helps to know if the module and the kernel you are using are compatible or not.

Aside from providing more information about a tool's functionality, modinfo can also be used to get information about why a tool is malfunctioning.

*How to add and remove modules with the **modprobe***

In some recent distributions of Linux, including the Linux Kali, the **modprobe** command is added to the LKM management. The **modprobe** command is used to add and remove modules from your kernel. To use this command to add a module, type in the following format:

kali >modprobe -a <module name>

To remove a module, type in the following format:

kali >modprobe-r <module to be removed>

One major advantage of using the **modprobe** command in the place of the **insmod** is that **modprobe** understands the importance of dependencies. As such, it takes all the dependencies function into account before adding or removing any module. Thus, **modprobe** command is safer and better than **insmod** command.

How to Insert and Remove a Kernel Module

Like the module, kernel modules can also be added and removed to make the system function properly. For instance, assuming you just installed a new video card and you need a driver for the card to function well, you would have to install the driver into the kernel. Installing the kernel makes the driver too strong for hackers to access. Now let's assume that the name of our driver is **ExpertHackerNewVideo**. The command to the driver would be in the format below:

kali >modprobe -a ExpertHackerNewVideo.

To test if this is working well, use the **dmesg** command.

To remove the driver, use the following command:

kali >modprobe -r ExpertHackerNewVideo

In conclusion, as effective as the LKM (loadable kernel module) are, they can serve as a major security threat.

Chapter Sixteen

Hashes, Passwords, And Encryption

As a hacker, you will often encounter hashes, passwords, and encryption. Hashing is a mathematical operation that is very simple to execute but very cumbersome to reverse. It is referred to as a *one-way* function.

A hash does not permit a user to decrypt the file with a definite key. However, this is not so for encrypted passwords. Encryption permits users to use a *two-way* function. It can be reversed. Your application stores the key when your password is encrypted. Therefore, if snoopers get the key as well as the encrypted text, they can effortlessly get the original password. Entering data for hashing is referred to as a *message,* while the output is referred to as the *message digest.*

In Kali Linux, the applications menu will show you a list of major password attack tools such as John, Crunch, Rainbowcrack, Wordlist, etc. You will see four classes, when you click the password attacks soon menu: Online attacks, Offline attacks, Passing the hash tools, and password profiling and Wordlist. It is quite simple to crack short passwords with simple strings of words or letters.

The online attacks menu encapsulates tools used to attack a live system and gain access to it. The offline attacks are the set of tools that takes the collection of passwords to match the password and the hash value. Passing the hash tools tries to obtain control of a password by getting the hash value with hash tools. Password profiling and Wordlist are tools that perform dictionary attacks.

John is a password cracking tool that has its own efficient modules for various hash types and device structures. John is community-based. Therefore, it provides support for more password hash types, which includes MacOS 10.4-10.6. salted SHA-1 hashes, Windows NTLM (MD4-based), and so on. This cracking tool is beneficial in the sense that it is very fast and available for various platforms.

Crunch is another tool that enables password cracking. Kali Linux supplies a tool to create a dictionary through Crunch. This tool helps you to generate password files. Also, you can create a list of passwords through Crunch and store the output in a text file.

Another great password cracking tool is rainbowcrack. It uses a unique type of time memory algorithm known as *trade off* to crack hashes. First of all, a rainbow table is created and then cranks hashes with a fast time memory *trade off* method. To crack windows NTLM(MD4-based), create a rainbow table using this command: root@kali:/usr/share/rainbowcrack# rtgen ntlmlower-alphaa 66038003355400.

To be a professional penetration tester, you need to make your client's system protected so as not to expose some confidential information, especially passwords. This is why cryptography has been designed to guard against dispersing secrets in a way that does not allow unauthorized persons to gain access to information. Cryptography entails encryption files or information by creating secret keys, and these keys are referred to as *symmetric* when they deal with encrypting information, however, when the keys are used to convey a secret key to a system to match the pair, they are referred to as *asymmetric*. Years back, cryptographers encrypted information through *cyphers*. Cyphers are used to conceal information by modifying the characters. Cyphers have some definite rules, and this makes it easy for anyone who understands the rules to decrypt the cypher data.

During the 1950s, the growth of modern computer systems altered the world of cryptography. During this period, different forms of algorithms came into existence.   V b However, they have been classified into two, *symmetric* and *asymmetric*. The clear distinction between both is that, while *symmetric* uses a single key to encrypt as well as decrypt information, *asymmetric* uses two keys (public and private keys)

Chapter Seventeen

The Logfile

Mastering how the log file works is an essential skill for all Linux users. The log file is where the user keeps all information about the activities that took place when the operating system and applications are run. The information stored in the log file includes security alerts and errors. While this tool is available to all users, there are some rules to observe **to** use it. This chapter examines how to use the log file and the rules guiding the use of the log file.

Things to Note About the Log File

There are few things to take note of when using the log file.

- As a hacker, you can use the log file as a trail to another person's identity and activities on a server, especially if the person is your target. However, the log file can also be used to trail your activities on someone else's system. Therefore, as a hacker, you should be careful of the information that can be gathered about your activities and methods. Hide all implicating information about you.

- Also, when securing a Linux system, as a hacker, the knowledge of how the Linux log file functions would help you to find out if the system has been once hacked. If it has, you would be able to find out who, why, and when the system was hacked.

This chapter covers how to configure the log file, remove and disable all evidence of your activities, and the daemon that is used to perform the log file functions.

The Rsyslog Logging Daemon

The name of the daemon used in Linux is **syslogd**. The daemon enables you to log events on your system automatically. There are different variations of syslogd. These include the **rsyslog** and **syslog-ng**. Although the different variations are used to carry out the same functions, their capacity and effectiveness differ. By default Linux Kali is built with Debian, and Debian comes with **rsyslog**. Therefore our focus in this chapter would be on the **rsyslog** tool.

The rsyslog Configuration File

Rsyslog, like every other application on Linux, is managed and configured by the plaintext located in the **etc/directory.** The configuration file for **rsyslog** is located at the **/etc/rsyslog.conf**. This file is documented in detail with comments explaining its uses. When you open the file and navigate down to line 50, you would find the Rule section. Here, you can set and delete any rule of your choice.

The **rsyslog** rule section has three basic formats. They include the **facility** keyword, the **priority** keyword, and the **action** keyword. The **facility** keyword is used to reference the program whose messages are being logged. The programs in the facility keyword include **kernel**, **mail,** or **lpr.** The **priority** keyword determines the type of message that would be a log for a program while the **action** keyword references the exact location to send the log.

Some codes can be used in place of all three keywords. For the facility keyword, the following codes can be used:

auth/authpriv authorization/security messages

cron Clock daemons

daemon Other daemons

lpr Printing system

kern Kernel messages

user Generic user-level messages

mail Mail system

However, to use all facilities, an asterisk (*) can be used in place of a word. If you need more than one but not all facilities, you can list the facilities you need, separating one facility from the other using a comma.

As already explained, the priority keyword is used to tell the system the type of message to log. In this keyword, codes are listed from the lowest priority - **debug** - to the highest priority - **panic**. Like the asterisk sign in the facility keyword, in priority, asterisk sign can also be used to indicate that the messages of all priority are logged. When you want to specify a priority, you would first log the message of that priority and then follow this by the message of the next priority. For instance, assuming you want to specify the priority code of **emerg**, the system would log the message of **emerg** and the next higher priority. The full list of the codes for priority include:

debug

info

notice

warning

warn

error

err

crit

alert

emerg

panic

Some codes like **warning, warn, error, err, emerge,** and **panic** are already out of dates and should not be used.

The last keyword to examine is the action. As already explained, the action is where the log is sent to. Generally, the log file is sent to the **/var/log** directory with a filename explaining the type of facility that is used to generate them. For instance, a log file generated with the **auth** file would be sent in this format: **/var/log.auth.log**. With this knowledge, the hacker can easily change where the files are located, the priorities, or even disable some logging rules.

How to Clean up Logs With logrotate

Leaving log files on the system for a time can consume all the space on the hard drive. In the same vein, deleting them too frequently would mean not having enough log files for future purposes. The best way to handle this is to use **logrotate**. Logrotate is a tool that can be used to balance these requirements. The logrotate rotates the log files by transferring some logs to a different location, leaving you with a clean log file for future use. The archived location would remain for some time before it cleaned off.

One of the keywords used to rotate the system is the **cron. Cron** employs the logrotate utility to carry out its actions. However, it is advisable that before using the **cron** tool, use the **/etc/logrotate.conf** file to configure the logrotate so that it can choose the number of times your log rotation occurs. During the rotate period, you can set the number of times you want to rotate log. The default setting is every four weeks. However, if you want the rotating to take a long period or you want to clear them quickly, change this setting. But if you want the log rotate to occur frequently **to** save more space, change the setting to rotate 1.

When the old file is rotated, a new one is created. After every rotation, old files are pushed toward the end of the chain, and more space is made available to create new log files. This implies that old files like **/var/log.auth** will become **/var/log.auth.1**, then **/var/log.auth.2**, and so on. If your rotating time is every four weeks, when old files push to no 4, the last old file will delete when a new rotate takes place.

How to Remove Evidence

Whenever you compromise any Linux log file, it is important to disable the log file and clean all evidence of your activities. This is to avoid any form of detections. To clear all evidence, open the log file and remove all details about your activities line by line. However, this method can be time-consuming and can leave errors like omitted lines. Errors like omitted lines can raise suspicion, and the deleted line can be recovered by an expert forensic investigator.

Therefore, the best way to remove all evidence is to **shred** log files using the **shred** tool. To understand how this shred command works, first, go to the **help** section and read how **shred** works. By itself, the shred command deletes the log file and overwrites it several times. The more time the file is overwritten, the more difficult it is to recover. Using the **shred** command can also be time-consuming.

The best way to reduce the time is to use any of these two tools. The **f** option and the **n** option. A shredded log file cannot be recovered by any expert.

How to disable log file

The simplest way to disable a log file is to stop the **rsyslog** daemon. To do this, enter the following command:

kali >service rsyslog stop

In conclusion, the log file can be used to track all the activities of a system. For hackers, the log file can be used to track identity and activities. This is why it is important to either shred the details in the log file or disable the log file.

Chapter Eighteen

Penetration Testing

Penetration testing is very paramount, most especially to companies. This is because a penetration tester can notify companies ahead of time against likely attacks. In other words, penetration testers operate between the attacker and the owner of the attacked data or information.

In order to perform this objective, the penetration tester needs to go through some stages. The first stage is for him to gather information about the computer; the second stage requires him to ascertain vulnerabilities. Once the penetration tester detects an attack coming, he then provides a report of vulnerability to stop such attacks.

A penetration tester must be granted authorization by the client before breaking into the system of an organization. They can use their tools written in Python or use other applicable tools in Kali Linux. It is, however, preferable you develop your own tools as you can learn many other things in the process. There are several tools you can obtain from the Linux library for penetration testing. Thus Python plays a pivotal role in penetration testing and networking at large.

Furthermore, Python has two levels of access to network service. They are:

- Low-level access

- High-level access

In low-level access, a software developer can use the essential socket functionality for the operating system using Python's libraries. Software developers can work with both connection-oriented and connectionless protocols for programming reasons. A penetration tester can also use high-level access from Python libraries to obtain application-level network protocols. These projects include FTP, HTTP, and so on.

Also, a penetration tester should check both the software and hardware components such as email servers, firewalls, DNS, web servers, proxy servers, web sites, and so on. The company will be vulnerable to attacks if those areas are weak.

Linux is very crucial to penetration testers because it is open and free. It has many distributions that are specifically meant for penetration testing, unlike Windows, which requires some tools to be installed before the test can be done. Besides, some tools do not work with Windows.

Moreover, Linux comes with the most recent Python version. Effortlessly, you can download any IDE like PyCharm. You can also use Python itself for penetration testing.

The activity of penetration testing is not limited to tracking of emails or port scanning or a target's address. To hide some private directories that your target wants to keep away from search engine searches, webmasters often keep *robot.txt* files in the webroot. This is referred to as *a robot exclusion standard*. A website informs the webroot about restricted sections through this standard.

Web roots are used specifically for clarifying web sites. It is very important to note that not all robots are good. There are also robots such as malware, email gatherers, spambots, and other robots that search for vulnerabilities in a web portal.

A vital tool used for penetration testing is the Nmap Network Scanner. This is also done through Python scripts. You will need to build up this scanner to detect open ports and observe whether there are vulnerabilities. Nmap is undoubtedly one of the most potent hacking devices, which also has powerful documentation.

Conclusion

Hacking is a skill that is often interpreted as cyber theft or crime. It is believed that hackers are bad people engaging in all sorts of digital criminal activities. As such, when the word hacking is mentioned, the reaction that follows is caution.

However, not all hackers are thieves. Generally, there are two types of hackers: the ethical hackers and non-ethical hackers. Ethical hackers are those who have a good understanding of hacking and use their knowledge for the safety of the company's system or an individual's system. The non-ethical hackers are the bad eggs among hackers. They are those that use their hacking knowledge for the ruin of a company or individual.

We have kept our explanations for the tool necessary to be an effective ethical hacker. To be an effective hacker, especially in the present world, you need to understand how Linux operates because Linux offers you a full package of all you need to carry out your work almost effortlessly. Linux is created with advanced applications that can help to boost your hacking skill.

Unlike any other operating system, there are several operating services Linux has made available to you. You can alter and manipulate text files or data to your satisfaction.

Linux also offers you the ability to know everything going on in each component of the operating system, whereas, an operating system such as Windows will hide some of its operations from you. This makes Linux more transparent and reliable than other operating systems. Linux also makes use of terminals and commands, which make a naturally long process to be easily accomplished. In other words, It provides shortcuts to get tasks done quickly.

Also, understanding the Linux operating system is crucial to carrying out excellent penetration testing. Linux makes it easy to check for vulnerability ports and ensures the security of files or data through hashes, passwords, or encryption. The skills, tips and tricks provided in this book will hopefully lead you on an exciting ethical hacking adventure!

www.ingramcontent.com/pod-product-compliance
Lightning Source LLC
LaVergne TN
LVHW022321060326
832902LV00020B/3594